I0007658

C++ FOR BEGINNERS:

LEARN IN A WEEK STEP BY STEP TO USE C ++
PROGRAMMING LANGUAGE WITH
PRACTICAL EXAMPLES FOR BEGINNERS.

Table of Contents

Description

C++ is a computer programming language. It was developed to make number improvements to the then C programming language. C is a structured programming language whereas C++ is an object-oriented programming language. This means that C introduced object-oriented programming features to the C programming language. Object oriented programming involves the treatment of items as objects. This is what C++ does. It is a case sensitive programming language, meaning that it differentiates between uppercase from lowercase letters. You have to be keen when naming and referring/calling objects in C++ so that you may call them using the right case according to their definition.

To program in C++, you only a text editor and the C++ compiler. The text editor will provide you with an environment where you will write your C++ programs. It is recommended that you give your C++ source files a .cpp extension to mark them C++ files. It is the default extension used by the C++ compiler. The purpose of the C++ compiler is to process your C++ source file to give you the result. There are many ways through which you can get this into your computer depending on the type of operating system you are using on your computer. For the case of the text editor, you can for the basic ones like Notepad on Windows and vim for Windows and Linux/Unix. Once you have assembled these, you can write, compile and execute C++ programs on your computer.

This guide will focus on the following:

- C++ Functions
- Operators
- Storage classes
- Identifiers
- Decision Control in C++
- Using Switch Statements
- Writing and Reading Files
- More on Functions & Data Types
- Constants and Literals
- Signed and Unsigned Data types
- Introduction to Classes
- Deeper Class Concepts
- Object Oriented Programming
- Improved Techniques
- Multithreaded Applications in C++... AND MORE!!!

Introduction

C++ is a general language that can work with a variety of huge systems, as well as smaller ones. It is a prominent language when creating commercial apps. There are large variety of items written in C++, these include:

- Operating systems like Linux and Mac OS X

- Games like World of Warcraft and the Diablo series

- Popular Wii, PlayStation & XBOX games

- Virtual Machines for programming languages (These languages include Python, Java, Rudy, PFP, Perl)

- Popular software like MS Office, Adobe Photoshop, Inventor and AutoCAD)

- Web Browsers (Chrome, Internet Explorer and Firefox)

- Many Apple iOS applications

This list proves that C++ is a general language that has the power to do almost anything.

If you're wondering if C++ will still be relevant tomorrow or in the next 10 years, the answer is YES!

C++ in conjunction with its predecessor C provide access to hardware and a high level of abstraction. It is the third most used language after C, which falls behind Java as the number one. As of now there is no rival in place to replace C++.

Chapter 1 : C++ Functions

A function refers to a set of statements that perform related tasks. Every program in C++ has at least one function, which is the **main()** function and it is possible for more functions to be defined within the program.

A C++ program can be subdivided into a set of functions. The way you sub-divide the code lies up to you, but it should be done in such a way that every function performs a certain task.

When such code is grouped together and given a name, it becomes easy for you to reuse the code calling and calling it again through the function name. Again, the code will become optimized since there will be no need for you to write it again. Suppose your goal is to check three numbers, 150, 230 and 450 to tell whether they are even or not. Without the use of a function, you will have to write the logic for the even number each time. This will be a repetition of code. However, by use of a function, you can write the logic only once and keep on calling it.

Function Declaration

The work of a function declaration is to tell the C++ compiler about the name of the function, its return type and parameters. To define a function in C++, we use the following syntax:

returnType functionName(dataType parameter**...**)

{

//function body code

}

From the above syntax, you can tell that a function definition is made up of a header and function body.

A function can return any value. The **returnType** denotes the data type of the value returned by the function. However, there are functions that will perform their tasks without returning values. In such a case, the return type should be *void*.

The **functionName** is the name of the function. The **functionName** together with the parameter list form the function signature.

See a parameter as a **placeholder**. When you invoke a function, you pass a value to the parameter. The value will be the actual parameter or argument. Note that each parameter is associated with a data type. Also, note that there are functions without parameters.

The function body should have statements defining what the function should when invoked.

Here is an example of a simple function:

```
#include <iostream>
using namespace std;
void myFunc() {

    static int x=0; //static variable

    int y=0; //local variable

    x++;

    y++;


    cout<<"x is: " << x<<" and y is: " <<y<<endl;
}
int main()
```

```
{
    myFunc();

    myFunc();

    myFunc();
}
```

The code should print the following output when executed:

We have defined a function named **myFunc()**. The function takes no parameters and it is of void type, meaning that it returns nothing. Within the body of the function, we have defined one static variable x and one variable y. Their values have been initialized to 0. We have then called the increment operator on each of these two variables.

We have ended the body of the function **myFunc()**. Within the **main()** method, we have invoked the function **myFunc()** three times. Note that no parameter values have been passed during the invocation as our function takes no parameter. Since x is a static variable, the statement **x++** will increase the value of x by 1 per invocation, meaning we will get 1, 2 and 3. This will be different for variable y as it has not been marked as static. It will return 1, 1 and 1 for the three invocations.

You now know why we have the above output.

Let us create an example of a function that takes in parameters:

```
#include <iostream>
using namespace std;
// declare the function maxNum()
int maxNum(int x, int y);
```

```cpp
int main () {

    // declare local variables

    int p;

    int q;

    int max;

    // call the function to get the maximum value.

    max = maxNum(5, 12);


    cout << "The maximum value is : " << max << endl;
    return 0;

}

// function returning the max between two numbers
int maxNum(int x, int y) {

    // local variable declaration

    int result;

    if (x > y)

        result = x;

    else

        result = y;

    return result;

}
```

The code should return the following as the result:

We began by declaring a function named **maxNum()** taking two integer arguments, x, and y. The function is of integer data type, meaning that its return value will be an integer. Within the **main()** method, we have invoked this function in the following line:

max = maxNum(5, 12);

What happens is that we have called the function and passed to it the value of the arguments. In the above line, the value of parameter x is 5 while that of parameter y is 12. Order is very important. The result will be assigned to the variable named **max**.

Lastly, we have implemented the logic for our function. We want our function to return the larger of the two integers that we pass to it. The largest integer will be stored in the variable result. If the value of x is greater than that of y, then x will become the result. If y is greater than x, then y will become the result. That is what we have done in the function body.

In our above call, the function compared 5 and 12. 12 was found to be the largest, hence, it became the result.

For any function that accepts arguments, it must declare the variables that will be accepting the values of the arguments. The variables are referred to as the **formal parameters** of the function.

The formal parameters exhibit similar behavior as other local variables in the function and their creation happens after entry into the function and they are destroyed upon exit.

There are various ways through which we can pass the values of the arguments to the function. Let us discuss these:

Call by Value

This mechanism involves copying of the actual values of the parameters to the formal parameters of the function. Any changes made to the parameters inside the function will have no impact on the argument.

This is the default parameter passing mechanism used in C++. This means that the code in the function cannot change the arguments used for calling the function. Let us create a simple example to demonstrate this:

```cpp
#include <iostream>

using namespace std;

void substitute(int value);

int main()

{

int value = 2;

substitute(value);

cout << "The value is: " << value<< endl;

return 0;

}

void substitute(int value)

{

value = 10;

}
```

The code should return the following output:

We have defined a function named **substitute()** that takes in one integer argument named **value**. In the implementation of the function, we have set the value to 10. However, in the **main()** method, we changed this to 2. That is why we have the above output. The pass by value was implemented in the following lines:

int value = 2;

substitute(value);

We initialized the value and passed the name to the function. That is how simple pass by value is.

Call by Pointer

This mechanism involves copying the address of the argument into the formal parameter. This address is then used to get the actual value of the argument inside the function. This means that if a change is done to the parameter, the argument will be affected.

To pass a value by pointer, the argument pointers should be passed to the functions similarly to any other value. This means that the function parameters should be defined as pointer types as demonstrated in the following snippet:

// defining a function to swap values.

void interchange(int *a, int *b) {

  int temp;

  *temp = *a; /* save value at address a */*

  *a = *b; /* put b into a */

  b = temp; / put a into b */

```
   return;

}
```

Remember that a pointer * points to a memory location.

Let us create a complete code that demonstrates how this works:

```
#include <iostream>
using namespace std;
// declare a function
void interchange(int *a, int *b);
int main () {
   // declare a local variable:
   int x = 5;
   int y = 12;


   cout << "Before the interachange, the value of x is :" << x <<
endl;


   cout << "Before the interachange, the value of y is :" << y <<
endl;
   /* call the function to interchange the values.
     * &x indicates pointer to x, that is, address of variable x and
     * &y indicates pointer to y, that is, address of variable y.
   */
```

interchange**(&x, &y);**

cout << "After the interchange, the value of x is :" << *x* << *endl*;

cout << "After the interchange, the value of y is :" << *y* << *endl*;

return 0;

}

// defining a function to swap values.

void interchange(int *a, int *b) {

int temp;

temp = *a; /* save value at address a */

*a = *b; /* put b into a */

b = temp; / put a into b */

return;

}

Through call by pointer, we were able to interchange the values stored in the two different addresses. The code returns the following upon execution:

Call by Reference

In call by reference, the reference of an argument is copied to the formal parameter. Inside the function, we use the reference to access the actual argument that has been used in the call. This is an indication that the changes that have been made to the parameter will affect the argument that is passed.

To pass a value by reference, the argument reference is passed to the functions similarly as any other value. This means that the function parameters have to be declared as reference types as demonstrated in the following example:

// define a function to interchange values

void interchange(int &a, int &b) {

   int temp;

   temp = a; /* store the value at address a */

   a = b;   /* put b into a */

   b = temp; /* put a into b */

   return;

}

Again, we have the **interchange()** function that swaps the two values. Let us now see how we can call the function and pass the arguments by reference:

#include <iostream>

using namespace std;

// declaration of a function:

void interchange(int &a, int &b);

int main () {

   // declaration of a local variable:

```cpp
int x = 5;

int y = 12;


cout << "Before the interchange, the value of x is :" << x <<
endl;


cout << "Before the interchange, the value of y is :" << y <<
endl;
/* call the interchange function to swap the values through
reference.*/

interchange(x, y);


cout << "After the interchange, the value of x is :" << x <<
endl;


cout << "After the interchange, the value of y is :" << y <<
endl;
   return 0;

}

// defining a function to interchange values

void interchange(int &a, int &b) {

   int temp;

   temp = a; /* store the value at address a */

   a = b;   /* put b into a */

   b = temp; /* put a into b */
```

return;

}

The code should return the following output upon execution:

That is how pass by reference works in C++.

Default Values for Parameters

After defining a function, it is possible for you to define the default values for the parameters. In such a case, the default value will be used as the value of the parameter when you call the function without passing the value of that parameter.

To assign default values for parameters, you use the assignment operator during the function definition. When no value is specified, that default value will be used as the value of the parameter. However, if you pass a value for the parameter, the default value will be ignored and the passed value will be used instead.

The following example demonstrates this:

```
#include <iostream>
using namespace std;
int product(int x, int y = 10) {
    int result;
    result = x * y;
    return (result);
}
int main () {
```

```
// declare a local variable:

int x = 12;

int y = 5;

int result;

// call the product function to multiply the values.

result = product(x, y);

cout << "The product is :" << result << endl;

// call the product function with one argument only

result = product(x);

cout << "The product is :" << result << endl;

return 0;
}
```

The code should return the following result when executed:

Consider the following statement extracted from the code:

int product(int x, int y = 10)

Above, we are defining a function named **product()** that takes two integer arguments, x, and y. If we don't pass a value for the parameter y during the function call, then the parameter y will be assigned a default value of 10.

The function has been called for the first time in the following line:

result = product(x, y);

Above, the value of x is 12 while that of y is 5. When the two are multiplied, we get a result of 60, hence the source of the first line in the above output. The default value for parameter y, which is 10, has been ignored because we have specified a value for the parameter during the call.

We have called the same function for the second time in the following line:

result = product(x);

Above, we have called the **product()** function but we have only passed one parameter to it, x. The value of x is still 12. Since we have not specified the value for the parameter y, its default value of 10 specified during the declaration of the function will be used. The two are multiplied to return a result of 120. The default value for the parameter has been used since we did not specify its value during the function call.

Chapter 2 : Operators

There are various types of operators available in C++. The operators help in carrying out various operations on the defined variables in a C++ program. Let's look at each of the operators in more detail.

Arithmetic operators

These are operators that are used to work with numbers. The most common operators are shown below.

Arithmetic operators

Operator	Operation
+	This is used to add two operands
-	This is used to subtract one operand from another
*	This is used to multiple two operands
/	This is used to divide one operand by another
%	This gives the remainder value after a division operator
++	This is used to increment a value by one
--	This is used to decrement a value by one

The following program is used to showcase the way we can use arithmetic operators.

```cpp
#include <iostream>
int main() {
  // Defining 2 operands
  int i=10;
  int j=3;

  std::cout << "The addition of the two operands is  " << i+j << std::endl;
  std::cout << "The subtraction of the two operands is  " << i-j << std::endl;
  std::cout << "The multiplication of the two operands is  " << i*j << std::endl;
  std::cout << "The division of the two operands is  " << i/j << std::endl;
  std::cout << "The remainder after division of the two operands is  " << i%j << std::endl;
  std::cout << "Incrementing operand one by one  " << i++ << std::endl;
  std::cout << "Decrementing operand two by one  " << j-- << std::endl;

  return 0;
}
```

With this program, the output is as follows:

The addition of the two operands is 13

The subtraction of the two operands is 7

The multiplication of the two operands is 30

The division of the two operands is 3

The remainder after division of the two operands is 1

Incrementing operand one by one 10

Decrementing operand two by one 3

Relational operators

These are operators that are used to determine the value of conditions based on the value of the operands. The relational operators possible in C++ are given below.

Relational operators

Operator	Operation
==	This is used to check if two operands are equal
!=	This is used to check if two operands are not equal
>	This is used to check if one operand is greater than the other
<	This is used to check if one operand is less than the other

>=	This is used to check if one operand is greater than or equal to the other
<=	This is used to check if one operand is less than or equal to the other

If a condition evaluates to true, then a value of 1 is returned else a value of 0 is returned.

The following program is used to showcase the way we can use relational operators.

```
#include <iostream>
int main() {
  // Defining 2 operands
  int i=10;
  int j=3;
  std::cout << "Is i equal to j = " << (i==j) << std::endl;
  std::cout << "Is i not equal to j = " << (i!=j) << std::endl;
  std::cout << "Is i greater than j = " << (i>j) << std::endl;
  std::cout << "Is i less than j = " << (i<j) << std::endl;
  std::cout << "Is i greater than or equal j = " << (i>=j) << std::endl;
   std::cout << "Is i less than or equal j = " << (i<=j) << std::endl;
   return 0;
}
```

With this program, the output is as follows:

Is i equal to j = 0

Is i not equal to j = 1

Is i greater than j = 1

Is i less than j = 0

Is i greater than or equal j = 1

Is i less than or equal j = 0

Logical operators

These are operators that are used to determine the value of conditions based on the value of the operands, where the operands are Boolean values. The logical operators possible in C++ are given below.

Relational operators

Operator	Operation
&&	This is the logical AND operator
||	This is the logical OR operator
!	This is the Logical NOT operator

Below is the table for the logical operators based on the value of the operands for the AND operator.

Relational operators - AND

Operand A	Operand B	Result
True	True	1
True	False	0
False	True	0
False	False	0

The following program is used to showcase the way we can use logical operators for the AND operator.

```cpp
#include <iostream>
int main() {
    // Defining 3 operands
    bool i=true;
    bool j=true;
    bool k=false;
// show casing the AND operator
    std::cout << "i AND j = " << (i && j) << std::endl;
    std::cout << "i AND k = " << (i && k) << std::endl;
    std::cout << "k AND i = " << (k && i) << std::endl;
    std::cout << "k AND k = " << (k && k) << std::endl;
    return 0;
}
```

With this program, the output is as follows:

i AND j = 1

i AND k = 0

k AND i = 0

k AND k = 0

Below is the table for the logical operators based on the value of the operands for the OR operator.

Relational operators - OR

Operand A	Operand B	Result
True	True	1
True	False	1
False	True	1
False	False	0

The following program is used to showcase the way we can use logical operators for the OR operator.

```
#include <iostream>
int main() {
    // Defining 3 operands
    bool i=true;
    bool j=true;
    bool k=false;
    // show casing the OR operator
```

```
    std::cout << "i OR j = " << (i && j) << std::endl;
    std::cout << "i OR k = " << (i && k) << std::endl;
    std::cout << "k OR i = " << (k && i) << std::endl;
    std::cout << "k OR k = " << (k && k) << std::endl;
    return 0;
}
```

With this program, the output is as follows:

i OR j = 1

i OR k = 0

k OR i = 0

k OR k = 0

Below is the table for the logical operators based on the value of the operands for the NOT operator.

Relational operators - NOT

Operand A	Result
True	0
False	1

The following program is used to showcase the way we can use logical operators for the NOT operator.

```
#include <iostream>
int main() {
    // Defining 2 operands
    bool i=true;
    bool j=false;
    // show casing the NOT operator
    std::cout << " NOT i = " << (!i) << std::endl;
    std::cout << "NOT j = " << (!j) << std::endl;
    return 0;
}
```

With this program, the output is as follows:

NOT i = 0

NOT j = 1

Assignment operators

These are operators that are used to make assignment operations easier. The assignment operators possible in C++ are given below.

Assignment operators

Operator	Operation
=	This is used to assign the value of an operation to an operand.

+=	This is used to carry out the addition and assignment operator in one go.
-=	This is used to carry out the subtraction and assignment operator in one go.
*=	This is used to carry out the multiplication and assignment operator in one go.
/=	This is used to carry out the division and assignment operator in one go.
%=	This is used to carry out the modulus and assignment operator in one go.

Now let's look at how we can implement these operators in further detail.

The following program is used to showcase the way we can use assignment operators.

```cpp
#include <iostream>
int main() {
   // Defining 3 operands
   int i=5;
   int j=10;
   int k;
// show casing the Assignment operators
   std::cout << "The value of i+j is " << (k=i+j) << std::endl;
   std::cout << "The value of i+=j is " << (i+=j) << std::endl;
   std::cout << "The value of i-=j is " << (i-=j) << std::endl;
   std::cout << "The value of i*=j is " << (i*=j) << std::endl;
   std::cout << "The value of i/=j is " << (i/=j) << std::endl;
   std::cout << "The value of i%=j is " << (i%=j) << std::endl;

   return 0;
}
```

With this program, the output is as follows:

The value of i+j is 15

The value of i+=j is 15

The value of i-=j is 5

The value of i*=j is 50

The value of i/=j is 5

The value of i%=j is 5

Bitwise operators

These are operators that are used to make bit operations on operands. The assignment operators possible in C++ are given below.

Bitwise operators

Operator	Operation
&	This copies a bit to the result if it exists in both operands
|	This copies a bit to the result if it exists in either operands
^	This copies a bit to the result if it exists in one operands but not in both
<<	Here the left operands value is moved left by the number of bits specified by the right operand
>>	Here the left operands value is moved right by the number of bits specified by the right operand

The following program is used to showcase the way we can use bitwise operators.

```cpp
#include <iostream>
int main() {
    // Defining 3 operands
    int i=5;
    int j=10;
    int k;
// show casing the bitwise operators
    std::cout << "Showcasing the & bit operator " << (i & j) <<
std::endl;
    std::cout << "Showcasing the | bit operator " << (i | j) <<
std::endl;
    std::cout << "Showcasing the ^ bit operator " << (i ^ j) <<
std::endl;
    std::cout << "Showcasing the << bit operator " << (i<<2)
<< std::endl;
    std::cout << "Showcasing the >> bit operator " << (i>>2)
<< std::endl;
    return 0;
}
```

With this program, the output is as follows:

Showcasing the & bit operator 0

Showcasing the | bit operator 15

Showcasing the ^ bit operator 15

Showcasing the << bit operator 20

Showcasing the >> bit operator 1

Chapter 3 : Storage classes

Within a given C++ program, the scope and the lifetime of the functions of variables defined by the storage class. The specifiers placed in front of the type which they modify. In C++, the following storage classes can be used.

- AUTO
- STATIC
- register
- mutable
- EXTERN

The auto Storage Class

For all of the local variables, the default of storage class is the auto storage class.
Example:

int mount;

auto int month;

In the examples given above there are two variables defined in a storage class which is the same for both. The auto can only be used with local variables.

The register Storage Class

If you wish to define the local variables and store them in the RAM instead of the register, you can use of the register storage class. This implies that the size of the variable will be equal to the maximum size of the register. This cannot have the & operator to it as there is no memory location for it.

Syntax:

register int miles;

You should only use these registers for the variables which require a quick access, like counters. You should keep in mind that when you define a register, it doesn't imply that the variable is stored in that register. The variable might get stored in that register basing on the implementation and hardware restrictions.

The Static Storage Class

Instead of creating and destroying local variable whenever it goes in and out of the scope, the static storage class will tell the compiler to store the local variable during its lifetime. So, if you want your local variables to keep their values during function calls, you should make those are local variables static.

The static modifier is not just limited to local variables, it can be applied to global variables as well. After this, the scope of that variable will be restricted to the file in which that variable is declared.

When you use a static on a data member of a class, only one copy of it will be shared by all the objects of that class. Here is an example.

Example:

```
#include <iostream>
// Function declaration
void func(void);
static int count = 10; /* Global variable */
main()
  while(count--)
  {
    func();
```

```
   }
   return 0;
// Function definition
void func( void )
   static int i = 5; // local static variable
   i++;
   std::cout << "i is " << i ;
   std::cout << " and count is " << count << std::endl;
```

When you compile and execute the above code, it will produce the following output.

i is 6 and count is 9

i is 7 and count is 8

i is 8 and count is 7

i is 9 and count is 6

i is 10 and count is 5

i is 11 and count is 4

i is 12 and count is 3

i is 13 and count is 2

i is 14 and count is 1

i is 15 and count is 0

The extern Storage Class

There are some global variables which are visible to all of the program files. The extern storage class can be used for giving the reference of these global variables which are visible to the program files. You cannot initialise the variable using the 'extern' because it will only point debatable name to a predefined storage location.

In cases where you have more than one files and you define a function or a global variable which other files can use, the extern where do you stay in a different file for giving the reference of The function or variable. In simple words, we use the extern for declaring a function or a global variables that is present in another file.

In cases where multiple files share the same functions or global variables, the extern modifier is used. Here is an example program.

Example:

First File: main.cpp

```
#include <iostream>

int count ;

extern void write_extern();

main()

  count = 5;

  write_extern();
```

Second File: support.cpp

```
#include <iostream>

extern int count;

void write_extern(void)

  std::cout << "Count is " << count << std::endl;
```

Here, in this program the count is declared in another file using the extern keyword. Now if you combine both of these files as given below.

$g++ main.cpp support.cpp -o write

A right executable program will be produced. Now try to execute it and check the result as given below.

$./write

Chapter 4 : Identifiers

Now let us move on to the identifiers in the program. These identifiers are used to identify multiple things, such as classes, modules, functions and variables within a block. An identifier is going to be a group of letters and numbers that you are able to name your program or your files and they must start with a letter, but can have any letter or number you want afterwards. There are no punctuation characters other than what you might see in a sentence that are allowed as identifiers. You will not see characters such as @,&,% or $, and the programming is case sensitive. That means YokoOno is different than Yokoono, yokoOno, and yokoono. Make sure that you are capitalizing only the letters that you should be capitalizing in your programs.

Though pretty much anything can be an identifier, there are some things that are reserved for keywords in C++, and can't be used as identifiers. These words are as follows.

asm		
Break	Bool	Auto
Char	Catch	Case
Const cast	Const	Class
Delete	Default	Continue

Dynamic cast	Double	Do
Explicit	Enum	Else
False	Extern	Export
Friend	For	Float
Inline	If	Goto
Mutable	Long	Int
Protected	Private	Namespace
Reinterpret cast	Register	Public
Signed	Short	Return
Static cast	Static	Sizeof
Template	Switch	Struct
True	Throw	This
Typeid	Typedef	Try
Unsigned	Unlon	Typename
Void	Virtual	Using
While	Wchar t	Volatile

Everything else is fair game when it comes to identifiers. Think of identifiers as usernames and passwords. Mix it up, but make sure that they are functional.

Trigraphs

Trigraphs are going to be sequences of three characters that will represent just one character. You will notice these because they are going to start out with two questions marks at the beginning. Seems a little redundant to use three characters when one will work, but the reason behind this is so you do not confuse the program with the meaning of the character, as many are similar.

Here are some frequently used trigraphs to give you an example of what we mean.

??=   #

??/   \

??'   ^

??([

??)   ]

??! |

??<   {

??>   }

??-   ~

Not all compilers support trigraphs due to their confusing nature, and most people try to stay away from them, however, it has been found that when you memorize trigraphs, you are less likely to mess up by hitting the wrong symbol in your function.

Whitespace

Moving on to whitespace. This is the empty lines in a program. Sometimes they contain comments, and these are known as blank lines. The compilers completely ignore them. Whitespace describes blanks, new lines, tabs, characters and comments. It is merely used to make your program look more organized and readable.

There should be at least one line of whitespace between the variable/identifier and the statement.

QUIZ

You thought that you could just waltz through this book without being tested on if you were paying attention? No cheating either! Just because you can peek at the answers does not mean that you should. You should take it just like a normal quiz to truly test your knowledge so you can figure out if you need to go back and re-read over some things. This is a short quiz, so you will be okay.

1. What is whitespace?

2. Fill in the blanks _____ <<x=y+1_>>

3. What are trigraphs?

4. Who Invented the C with Classes language?

5. What is the header used in most functions?

Answers

1. The blank spaces or comments that the compiler ignores

2.Cout <<x=y+1;>>

3.A sequence of three characters that represent a single character

4.Bjarne Strousup

5.<iostream>

Chapter 5 : Decision Control in C++

The next topic that we are going to discuss is how to work with the conditional statements or the 'decision control' statements. There are times when you are working on a program, and you want to make sure that it is capable of making some decisions for you even when you're not there. This could happen when you would like the user or another programmer to put in some information, and then you want the program to respond based on the conditions that you set.

You can get the program to act a certain way based on the conditions that you add to the code. The decision making capability is a great way to ensure that the program does what you would like it to do even though it is a bit more complicated, there is a ton of times when you might want to add this to your code so learning it at this point can be a great idea.

There are a few different types of decision control statements that you can work with. For example, you can choose to go with one that only allows you to get one answer and call it right. There are conditional statements that will give out an answer based on the various answers that the user will put in. Or you could end up with one that gives out a list, like a menu of items and you can let the user pick from there.

Switch statements

The first type of conditional statements that you can work with is the switch statements. These statements can help you out a lot because they will allow you to check out whether your variable has an equal value against the other values or the other cases that you outlined in your code. The variable that you would be checking in here would be compared against a variety of cases by the statement. A good example of the syntax that you can use to create one of these switch statements is this:

Switch(expression){

case constant-expression:
statement(s);

break; //optional
case constant-expression:
statement(s);

break; //optional
//you can add in as many of these case statements as you would
like
Default: //Optional
statement(s);

}

When you are working with the switch statements, there are some rules that you have to follow to make them work inside of your code. First, the expression that you use with the switch statement should be either an enumerated or an integral class type. In addition to this, it can also belong to a class that has a conversion function. The good news is that when you are working with C++, there isn't a limit to how many of these case statements that you can add into this syntax so you can either make it long or short depending on what your code wants. The important thing to remember here is that you need to add in a colon as a value to each one that you want to use as well.

Once the variable finds a value that it is equal to, it will just keep on running until it finds a way to break the statement that you wrote. When the system finally finds this break statement, the switch will stop whatever it is that it's currently doing. Then, the control flow is going to pass on to the next part of the code. You do not need to add in a break statement to the cases. If you do not have one of these break statements, your control flow will just pass on to the next part automatically.

The 'if' statements

The next type of conditional statements that you can work with is known as the 'if' statement. One of the most basic things that you can create when it comes to conditional statements, is the if statement. These are based on a true or false statement. If the system decides that the input matches up to the conditions that you set, it is true, and the program is going to run the part that you added to it. For example, if you set it up so that the system asks what 2 + 2 is and the user puts in the right answer of 4, then this would be seen as true and the message that you pick, something like 'That is correct!' will show up on the screen.

Any time that you have the user input some kind of information and if the information they added meets up or complies with your conditions, then it will proceed to show up the statement or other things that you add into the code. But what is going to happen if the user puts in the wrong answer? If the user puts in that 5 is the answer to the question, 'What is 2 + 2?' then it will fail to meet the conditions that you set and the program will see this as false.

Since the if statement is one of the most basic forms of the conditional statements, you will find that it is not capable of handling a false answer all that well. If the user puts in any number that is not 4 as the answer for the question that we had placed, then the if statement will see this as false, it will leave the screen as blank, and nothing else will happen. This could be a problem for a lot of the codes that you want to write, and this is why you won't always find yourself working with the if statements.

The 'if' else statements

You will have various issues you'll have to fix if the user ends up putting in the wrong answer and the program sees this as a false statement based on the conditions that set in the code. This is where the 'if else' statement comes into play.

The if-else statement can be put to work in a variety of situations. Not only does it allow for the user to put in an answer that may not meet your conditions, but there are also times when you may want it to let the user pick from a few different options to start with. The if-else statement can help you to do all of this and the syntax for this is pretty simple. To create an if else statement, copy this example of the syntax:

if(boolean_expresion)

{

//statement(s) will execute if the boolean expression is true
}

Else

{

// statement(s) will execute if the boolean expression is false
You can then add in as many of these points into the if else statement as you would like. If you want to work on creating your own program that is capable of setting apart various people into five or six different age groups, is a task you can accomplish with the help of these if-else statements. You just need to add in some more of the 'else' keywords to make this happen.

So, let's take a look at how all of this will work and keep it really simple. Let's say that you are making a program that requires a user to solve the equation, 2 + 2. If the person guesses the right answer and inputs 4, you will be can set it up so that the first part is the true statement and then the message that you created to inform the user was right will come up on the screen. But, if your user puts in the wrong answer, or anything other than 4, then the program will assess that the answer is false based on the conditions that you set. Instead of going blank though, it is possible for you to add another option and get another statement, such as 'Sorry, that is incorrect' to come up on the screen.

As you can see, this gives you a lot of freedom when it comes to the things that you can have your program do. You can keep it as simple just like the example that we did above, or you can add in some various other things to make it more sophisticated and to also ensure that it's compatible so it can work with the code you're writing.

Another thing that you want to keep in mind when it comes to working with these if statements, is that you can add in some more of these if-else statements if needed and it is even possible to add in some of these if else statements inside of each other. This makes it pretty complex for someone who is just getting started, but with a bit of practice and patience to learn how to use the syntax, you will find that it will add a ton of power and flexibility to this process and will make it so much easier to do some of the various tasks that you would like your code to accomplish.

Working with the if statements and the if else statements can make your coding experience so much better. It allows the system to make decisions based on what the user is putting into the system rather than having to be there yourself always and doing it manually every time. Make sure to try out a few of these different types of statements and see how they work within your code and keep practicing on using these statements so you can discover the various functions they can fulfill.

The 'elif' statements

Another option that you can work with is the elif statements. These statements will allow you to take things to the next level. This will allow you to go a little bit further with your and make your program even better. These elif statements will list out the options that you would like to be available for your user. Think about it like a menu in a game. You can list out a few different things on a menu and let the user pick which one they would like to go with.

This is a great option because you can add a lot of functionality to the code that you are working on. The user will have the freedom to pick from the different options that you set out for them, and you can even add in a catch-all to make sure that you can track if the user does not like any of the results that you are providing to them.

You can add in as many parts to this as you would like. Sometimes you can only add in just a few options and other times you can make a long list that will give the user a lot of choices. You are also able to add in some statements for what the user will see if they pick each option. The statement that you will add here may vary based on how you are using the conditional statements inside of your own code.

For example, let's say that you want to put up a game where you would like to allow the user to go through and pick out the type of pizza that they would like to use. You could list out four types of pizza, such as cheese, pepperoni, veggie, and sausage. The user will pick from those pizzas, and then the corresponding statement that you set up would execute once the user has made a choice. You can even set it up so that there is another option for them not to get any pizza and maybe just choose a drink and that can be the catch-all in case the user does not want any of the pizza choices that you have listed.

As you can imagine, there are a lot of different options that you can go with when you're trying to use the elif statement. You have the freedom to add in as many or as few of these options as you would like to make your program work.

There are so many ways that you can work with the conditional statements. These statements are really useful and will help you with making your program work the way you want it to. You can get it to make decisions for you and even get it to behave the way that you would like. Make sure to try out a few of these different options so you can understand exactly how they work and to learn how they can be used to add more functionalities to the code you're doing.

Chapter 6 : Using Switch Statements

Using the switch selection statement is the last thing you need to learn as a novice in C++. The switch statement works by checking the value of constant expressions and running a group of statements or cases. Cases are then closed using break statements.

The syntax for initializing a switch statement is switch (expression) and the cases to be included will be enclosed in curly braces ({}). The expression is basically the identifier of the constant to be used in the switch selection statement.

The syntax for creating cases is case constant: followed by the group of statements to be executed and the break statement.

The purpose of using the switch selection statement is slightly similar to using if-else statements. The main difference is that switch selection statements are limited to constants. Moreover, you can easily create a number of different possibilities using a switch selection statement.

For example, when creating choices using if-else statements, you need to create multiple if or else if statement blocks for each condition. On the other hand, you can set as many cases as you like when using the switch selection statement. Also remember that the default label is optional.

Here is the typical example of a switch selection statement:

switch (n) // in this particular example, the constant value of x is checked

> *case 1:*
>> *cout << "The value of 'N' is 1";*
>> *break;*
>
> *case 2:*
>> *cout << "The value of 'N' is 2";*
>> *break;*
>
> *case 3:*
>> *cout << "The value of 'N' is 3";*
>> *break;*
>
> *default:*
>> *cout << "Unable to determine the value of 'N'";*

Notice that unlike case statements, you no longer need to use the break statement for default. Without the break statement, any other statements – even those within different cases – will be executed until another flow control statement is used or until the switch ends.

Finally, remember that due to its limitations, switch selection statements are best used only for constants with integer and character values. The use of logical operators is not possible when initializing switches or declaring cases, although they can be used inside the statement block. Using switch selection statements when working with strings may also be possible by using hash values, but it is nowhere near as efficient as using if-else statements when it comes to strings.

Here is an example of a switch statement to help you understand it further:

```cpp
#include <iostream>

int main ( )
        std::cout << "Would you like to continue (yes or no)?\n";

        char response = 0;

        std::cin >> response;

        switch (response)

        {

                case 'a':

                        return true;

                case 'b':

                        return false;

                default:

                        std::cout << "Your response is undetermined.\n";

                        return false;

        }
```

Running this program will yield to an output of:

Would you like to continue (yes or no)?

Your response is undetermined.

When writing a program with a *switch statement*, see to it that your case constants are distinct. If you do not want to include a default statement, you may skip it.

Activity: Color Program using Flow Control Statements

Knowing the functions of flow control statements is meaningless if you don't know how to apply them in a program. To make sure you're keeping up with everything you've learned so far, you need to see these statements in action. Feel free to create any changes to these codes and try running them using your IDE.

By now you should already have a working IDE for learning C++. If you're a student, you should be able to request a copy from your instructor. Below is an example program that utilizes a switch statement integrated within a loop.

```
#include <iostream>
using namespace std;
int main ()
        bool valid = true; // Section 1
        char color;
        cout << "Welcome. Choose a primary color!\n
        Please enter R for Red, B for Blue, and Y for Yellow";
        while (valid) // Section 2
        {
```

```cpp
cin >> color;
if (color == 'b')  // Section 3
{
        color = 'B';
}
else if (color == 'r')
        {
                color = 'R';
        }
        else if (color == 'y')
                {
                        color = 'Y';
                }
switch (color) // Section 4
{
case 'B':
        cout << "You chose blue!";
        valid = false;
        break;
case 'R':
        cout << "You chose red!";
        valid = false;
        break;
case 'Y':
        cout << "You chose yellow!";
        valid = false;
        break;
```

```
                default:

                        cout << "Please input a valid answer.";

                }

        }

        return 0;
```

SECTION 1 – INITIALIZING VALUES IN THE PROGRAM

The first section contains your standard initialization statements. Notice that the data types char and bool are used since they fit the functions required in this program most appropriately. Section 1 also contains the initial output code in order to prompt the user to choose between any of the three primary colors.

SECTION 2 – CHECKING FOR A VALID ANSWER

Remember that the statements inside a while loop will execute when the expression is evaluated to be true. Once the user provides a valid input, this value will be changed to false – thereby ending the loop.

SECTION 3 – CHECKING FOR LOWERCASE INPUT

In this section, lowercase input is changed to uppercase. For example, when the user inputs lowercase 'y', the uppercase value 'Y' is saved instead. Keep in mind that logical operators can't be used when declaring cases in switch statements. Therefore, inserting lowercase answers – regardless if they correspond to a valid answer or not – will automatically result in a default.

SECTION 4 – THE SWITCH STATEMENT

Finally, section 4 contains a switch statement that executes different cases based on the user's input. Again, remember that cases are closed with the break statement. Also make sure to include a statement to change the Boolean value of valid to false, otherwise the while loop will repeat infinitely.

Chapter 7 : Writing and Reading Files

This concept, known as *file i/o*, is one of the most essential things to understand in programming. In fact, in your first and second semesters of an official programming course, they'll be talking rather extensively about *how* to input and output files.

So, let's talk about that for just a brief second - input streams and output streams.

However, input and output streams are just a vague idea; more symbolic of the idea of data flow than anything else. For example, an input stream just signifies that data is being taken *in* to the program. On the other hand, an *output* stream just signifies that data is flowing out *from* the program. This is all that input and output streams signify at their core.

With that said, this idea actually has quite a bit of meat to it that you really need to recognize. For example, what *defines* data? More importantly, where all can data *come from*?

One of the key places which data comes from is the file system. This is actually the place for long term storage of data on a computer, so it's incredibly important that you know how to work around it and use it to your full advantage. You aren't a good programmer if you don't know how to work with a file system, and that's just the long and short of it.

File input and output serves a lot of uses. You don't always recognize these uses, though. Any time that you need to save data in order to use at another point, or even take in essential data from the computer itself, you're going to be using file input and output algorithms. Easy peasy.

Let's talk more, then, about how this applies to C++ specifically. How can we use this discussion on file input and output in order to do something productive regarding C++? The first thing that we're going to want to discuss is file *output*.

You can access the file input and output streams in the same exact way. All that you do is include the fstream library in your program, like so:

#include <iostream>

#include <fstream>
using namespace std;

int main() {

// ...

}

The first thing that you're going to need to do from here will be to open a file for writing. To do this, you can just instance a new output stream, shortened to *ofstream*. Like so:

int main() {

ofstream my_file;

}

The next thing that we need to do is *open* a file. Now, let it be noted that you can create a vague *fstream* variable just opening the file stream instead of creating a variable meant to either take in or push out information (ifstream or ofstream respectively). If you do this, then you can do much more with your file through the open function. ifstream, ofstream, and fstream all have separate open methods. However, fstream allows you to define *how* you're going to open a given file. These methods are like so and may be passed with the following syntax:

fstream my_file;

my_file.open("filename.txt", fileMethod);

In these cases, the fileMethod may be any of the following:

ios::out

This is functionally the same as *ofstream*. It just declares that you're opening a file, for writing, of the given file name. If a file already exists with that name then the file will be overwritten with the new data.

ios::in

This is functionally the same is *ifstream*. This allows you to read data in from a given file with the specified name. Super easy!

ios::app

This allows you to *append* data to a given file. This means that you can actually add text to the end of the file name rather than just overwriting the file. This can be immensely useful in a lot of cases where you need to add data to an already existing file.

ios::binary

This allows you to open a file in binary mode which allows you to perform both input and output operations upon a given file. However, the usage of this specific argument is rather advanced and goes beyond the scope of this book, so we aren't going to worry too much about it and what you can do with it.

Let's say now that we've opened a file called *numbers.txt*. Our main method would now look like this:

int main() {

ofstream my_file;

my_file.open("numbers.txt");

}

Since we have an *ofstream* file which defaults to ios::out, we don't have to specify an argument for input or output. It automatically knows to use the ios::out parameter.

Now that we have opened this file stream, we can write text to the file just like we would for the console output stream! It's incredibly intuitive and it isn't worth fretting over. Just see for yourself. The primary caveat is that we need to test that the file is open. We can do this with an if statement. From there, we can actually read out whatever information we want into the file. Let's read a bunch of numbers into it and separate these numbers by a newline. The code would then look something like this:

#include <iostream>

#include <fstream>

using namespace std;

int main() {

ofstream my_file("numbers.txt");

// you can automatically open the file by providing the filename

// as an argument when creating it.

if (my_file.is_open()) {

my_file << "2\n3\n4\n5\n6\n7\n8\n9\n";

}

}

However, there is one more thing that we need to do - we must *close* the file after we're finished with it. This ensures that the file doesn't become corrupted through any series of events. This is always good practice. You can do this within the if statement, like so:

```
if (my_file.is_open()) {

// code

my_file.close();

}
```

Now, the last thing we want to do is a very basic form of exception handling. Let's go ahead and define an *else* statement for this function that will tell the user if my_file is *not* open that there was a problem opening the file. We could actually get more nuanced with it and see if the file exists at all, but this is a pretty good place to start, all things considered.

```
if (my_file.is_open()) {

// code goes here

my_file.close();

} else {

cout << "File could not be opened.\n";

}
```

For now, our code looks a bit like this:

```
#include <iostream>

#include <fstream>

#include <string>

// since we're working with strings, we have to define a string
include
```

```
using namespace std;

int main() {

ofstream my_file("numbers.txt");

if (my_file.is_open()) {

my_file << "2\n3\n4\n5\n6\n7\n8\n9\n";

my_file.close();

} else {

cout << "File could not be opened.\n";

}

}
```

Now, we're going to read each line from that file, add 1, and print it out to console. The process for reading a file is relatively simple. Firstly, you need to open the file with an input stream. Then, you need to use the getline method. The getline method returns a true or false value - true if there's a line to get, false if there isn't. It takes two arguments: the *input stream* and the *target string*.

The syntax for the getline method is like so:

```
getline(istream, targetString);
```

Let's go ahead and define two new variables where we defined our output stream. Let's define an input stream variable - but, notably, we aren't going to open it yet, so we aren't going to send the file name as an argument. Let's also define a string variable that we can store the current line to. Our variables should now look like this:

```
ofstream my_file("numbers.txt");
```

```cpp
ifstream read_in;

string current_line;
```

Now, we can actually get to work doing something with all of this. After the file has been closed and we've defined our else statement, let's go ahead and open the numbers file with the input stream:

```cpp
read_in.open("numbers.txt");
```

Now, we can read in all of the text while the file is open.

```cpp
if (read_in.is_open())

{

while ( // there is a line to get )

{

// internal logic with each line

}

read_in.close();

} else {

cout << "File could not be opened.";

}
```

Allow us to insert our getline method into our while loop. For as long as this method returns *true*, the loop will execute. When it returns false - i.e., when there are no more lines to return - the loop will terminate, and the file will close.

```cpp
while (getline(read_in, current_line)) {

// internal logic with each line
```

```
}
```

Now, we want to start doing some parsing. What we're going to do is convert each string read in to an integer and add 1, then we're going to print that number to the console. To do this, we also need to define an int variable called *my_int*. Afterward, the logic within the while loop looks like so:

```
my_int = atoi(current_line.c_str());

my_int++;

cout << my_int << "\n";
```

So with that, we now have a file input loop that looks like this:

```
while (getline(read_in, current_line)) {

my_int = atoi(current_line.c_str());

my_int++;

cout << my_int << "\n";

}
```

There we go! The whole of our code will look like this:

```
#include <iostream>

#include <fstream>

#include <string>

using namespace std;

int main() {

ostream my_file("numbers.txt");

int my_int;
```

```cpp
string current_line;

ifstream read_in;

if (my_file.is_open()) {

my_file << "2\n3\n4\n5\n6\n7\n8\n9\n";

my_file.close();

} else {

cout << "File could not be opened.\n";

}

read_in.open("numbers.txt");

if (read_in.is_open()) {

while (getline(read_in, current_line) {

my_int = atoi(current_line.c_str());

my_int++;

cout << my_int << "\n";

}

read_in.close();

} else {

cout << "File could not be opened.\n";

}

}
```

Easy enough! That's what your final file *could* look like. Do remember our discussion on *fstream* and arguments, though. Using that knowledge, we can actually clean our file up like so.

```cpp
#include <iostream>

#include <fstream>

#include <string>

using namespace std;

int main() {

int my_int;

string current_line;

fstream my_file;

my_file.open("numbers.txt", ios::out);

if (my_file.is_open()) {

my_file << "2\n3\n4\n5\n6\n7\n8\n9\n";

my_file.close();

} else {

cout << "File could not be opened.\n";

}

my_file.open("numbers.txt", ios::in);

if (my_file.is_open()) {

while (getline(my_file, current_line) {

my_int = atoi(current_line.c_str());
```

```
my_int++;

cout << my_int << "\n";

}

my_file.close();

} else {

cout << "File could not be opened.\n";

}

}
```

With that, we've covered an essential computer science topic and really started to get to the bottom of it. We can now move from this topic onto our final topic - object-oriented programming.

Chapter 8 : More on Functions & Data Types

Separate functions outside of the main function can also be created in the same program. However, don't forget that only themain ()function is called upon automatically when running a program. All other functions are called using the identifiers associated with them when they were initialized.

A simple way to utilize separate functions is to pass arguments through them and return a resulting value. Basically, functions can extract values from the main function (or any other function that calls it) and save them on the specified parameters when the function was initialized.

Calling Functions
Here is a simple example on how to call other functions from the main function:

```
#include <iostream>
using namespace std;
int distribute (int x, int y) // this is the distribute function
        int z;
        z = x / y;
        return z;
int main () // this is the main function
        int a;
        int b;
        int c;
```

```
cout << "How many pies are there?\n";
cin >> a;
cout << "How many people are there?\n";
cin >> b;
c = distribute (a, b); //the function is called here
cout << "Each person will receive " << c << " pie(s)
each.";
}
```

In the main function, the user is prompted to insert the number of pies as well as the number of people to share the pies. Upon entering the appropriate numbers, the main function calls thedistributefunction to divide the number of pies with the number of people to calculate the most even distribution of pies.

A function can use the return statement to go back to where it was called. Notice how the values ofaandb from the main function is sent to the distribute function where the valueofc will be evaluated. Take a look at the diagram below:

$\uparrow\uparrow$
| |int distribute (int x, int y)

c = distribute (a,   b)

In the distribute function, the value ofzis then returned using the return statement.

Finally, the return statement ends the called function and returns the programto where the function was originally called. In this particular example, the program returns to the point after the linec = distribute (a, b);-- where the final value of c will be printed.

Take note that his is only a simple example to illustrate what you can do with multiple functions. It is also possible to work with several functions that call upon each other in a chain. But with functions as small as the example given above, it is far more desirable to simply include the statements of the other function inside the main function.

Arrays

An array can be used to save a large amount of data while maintaining a functional structure. In arrays, data are contiguously stored and operates under the same name. In other words, arrays are basically groups of data using the same identifier. Each data contains values that can be accessed or referenced to individually.

Here is the syntax for declaring arrays:

type name [index];

Just like when declaring functions and variables, you always start by identifying the data type you wish to associate with an array. Next is the array 'name' or the identifier you wish to associate with the array. Finally, you have to specify the number of data that can be stored in the array. This should be an integer and must be enclosed in brackets ([]). This is also syntactically known as the index.

Keep in mind that the index does not represent a value; rather, it represents how many values can actually exist inside the array. These values are also called as elements. For example, if you wish to declare an array that can contain a total of 10 elements with integer values, you can use thesyntax int myarray [100];.

This is why arrays containing characters were used. To declare arrays that stores character data, simply declare it using the syntaxchar myarray [y];. In this case, the valueyrepresents the number of individual characters that can be stored inmyarray.

Setting Values to Elements

When an array is first declared, all elements inside it will not contain any value. There are two ways for elements to receive values. One, a value may be given to an element upon initializing an array. Two, a value may be given to an element by individually referencing its index in a statement later on.

Here is the correct syntax for setting values for the elements of an array upon initialization:

int myarray [10] = { 1, 3, 5, 7, 9, 11, 13, 15, 17, 19 };

It is important to remember that the indices of an array always start with 0. If you create an array with 10 elements, the indices referring to each element are 0, 1, 2, 3, 4, 5, 6, 7, 8, and 9. Based on this example, the values of each element inmyarray are:

myarray [0] = 1

myarray [1] = 3

myarray [2] = 5

myarray [3] = 7

Of course, you may also set these values using statements after declaring an array. For example, you can set the value of myarray [1] to 2 using the syntax:

myarray[1] = 2;

Accessing an element is also as simple as referencing it using its index. For example, if you wish to access the value of the fifth element ofmyarray, you can simply use the expressionmyarray[4].

When initializing arrays, you can always leave the index blank (the number between the brackets). If this is used, the compiler automatically adjusts the value of the index to the number of elements entered upon initialization. For example, using the syntaxint myarray [] = {1, 2, 3, 4, 5};automatically sets the index to [5].

Array Dimensions

A standard array using one index is considered as a 1-dimensional array. However, you can also create multidimensional arrays which utilize 2 or more indices. To help you understand this, visualize a 1-dimensional array as a graph with a single row:

	[0]	[1]	[2]	[3]	[4]
myarray	1	3	5	7	9

In a 1-dimensional array, a single index may only contain 1 value. However, you can also create an array within an array to store more value in a single index. This is also referred to as a bidimensional array.

For example, you can declare a 5x5 bidimensional array using the syntax:

int myarray [5][5];

This array can be visualized as:

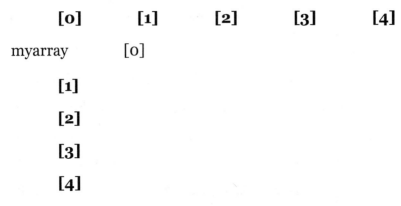

It is also possible to use as many dimensions as you can when using arrays. However, bear in mind that each new dimension you add in an array significantly increases the amount of memory needed for it. When it comes to arrays, there is hardly any application for anything beyond 2-dimensional.

When referencing an element from a 2-dimensional array, you should include both indices from each dimension. For example; say you want to refer to the element marked in the array below:

[0]	[1]	[2]	[3]	[4]
myarray	*[0]*			

[1]	y
[2]	x

The element marked with 'x' is the elementmyarray [2][1]while the element marked with 'y' is the elementmyarray [1][2].

As far as applications go, arrays are effective for creating structured data and for representing 2-dimensional fields such as the playing boards for minesweeper, chess, and tic tac toe.

Passing Arrays to Other Functions

In the C++ language, there is no means of passing an entire array to another function and use them for arguments. However, function parameters can accept an array's address, meaning it can access the local values from its source. This is essentially the same process and does in fact, save memory by eliminating the need to save a new set of data.

In order for this to happen, an array type can be declared in a function's parameters – but only with an undefined index. In other words, this simply means the function parameter may accept any array sent to it regardless of its index size. However, the data type of an array to be sent must match that of the function's parameter.

For example, you can initialize a function with the following syntax:

void arrayfunction (int array[])

For example, you can initialize an array from a separate function using the syntax:

int arraytopass [] = {1, 2, 3};

Next, you can pass these values to arrayfunction using the statement:

arrayfunction (arraytopass);

Here is an example program with a function that prints the elements of an array from the main function:

```
#include <iostream>
using namespace std;
void arrayfunction (int myarray[], int sequence)
        for (int n = 0; n < sequence; ++n)
                cout << myarray[n] << " ";
        cout << "\n";
int main ()
        int arraytopass[] = {1, 2, 3, 4, 5};
        arrayfunction (arraytopass, 5);
```

In this particular example, the arrayarraytopass[]from the main function was passed toarrayfunctionas well as a matching integer value forsequence. To explain the relevance of these expressions, take a look atarrayfunction. Here is a closer look on the following statements:

arrayfunction (int myarray[], int sequence)

When initializingarrayfunction,the parameters formyarray[]andsequencewere used. Thesequencevalue is important since the function uses a loop that runs depending on the number of elements. Since the number of elements will be decided from a separate function (in this example, the main function), the value for the variablesequencewas left blank upon initializingarrayfunction. Thus, it is open to receiving any integer value from another function.

int arraytopass[] = {1, 2, 3, 4, 5};

arrayfunction (arraytopass, 5);

In the main function, the arrayarraytopass[] was initialized along with its elements. Notice the statement immediately after the initialization statement for the array. This is wherearrayfunction was called. This is also wherethe expressions from the main function that matches the parameters inarrayfunction were passed. Take a look at the diagram below:

⇑⇑void arrayfunction (int myarray[], int sequence)

arrayfunction (*arraytopass*,   *5*);
Finally, the value ofsequencecorresponds to the number of elements inarraytopass[]. This is because the function utilizes a basic decaying loop that outputs each element in the array in a sequential manner. In this particular example, you should set the value ofsequence to 5 since there is a total of 5 elements in the array.

Chapter 9 : Constants and Literals

A constant is referred to a value that cannot be changed. The literal is the most common type of constant. These are used to specify a type of literal. There are different types of literals which are classified below.

An integer literal can be a decimal, octal, or hexadecimal constant. An integer literal can also have a suffix that is a combination of U and L, for unsigned and long, respectively.

The following program is used to showcase the way we can define constants.

```cpp
#include <iostream>
int main() {
    //This is used to define a floating constant value
    const float f=3.14;
    //This is used to define an integer constant value
    const int i=3;
    std::cout << "The value of the floating constant is " << f <<
std::endl;
    std::cout << "The value of the integer constant is " << i <<
std::endl;
    f=4.145;
    i=4;
    return 0;
}
```

With this program, the output is as follows:

The value of the floating constant is 3.14

The value of the integer constant is 3

Now let's look at another example which can confirm our understanding of constants.

The following program is used to showcase an error condition when using constants.

```
#include <iostream>
int main() {
    //This is used to define a floating constant value
    const float f=3.14;
    //This is used to define an integer constant value
    const int i=3;
    std::cout << "The value of the floating constant is " << f << std::endl;
    std::cout << "The value of the integer constant is " << i << std::endl;
    f=4.145;
    i=4;
    return 0;
}
```

With this program, the output is as follows:

error: assignment of read-only variable 'f' f=4.145;

error: assignment of read-only variable 'i' i=4;

We rightly so get an error because we are trying to change the value of constants which cannot be changed as per their definition.

Now let's look at the use of literals. We have different types of literals and let's look at each one of them in more detail.

Integer literals

The following program is used to showcase the use of integer literals.

```
#include <iostream>
int main() {
    //This is used to define an unsigned integer literal
    int i=100U;
    //This is used to define a long integer literal
    int i1=100L;
    //This is used to define an unsigned long integer literal
    int i2=100UL;
    std::cout << "The value of the unsigned integer literal is "
    << i << std::endl;
    std::cout << "The value of the long integer literal is " << i1
    << std::endl;
    std::cout << "The value of the unsigned long integer literal
    is " << i2 << std::endl;
    return 0;
}
```

With this program, the output is as follows:

The value of the unsigned integer literal is 100

The value of the long integer literal is 100

The value of the unsigned long integer literal is 100

The following program is used to showcase how to use hexadecimal and octal literals.

```
#include <iostream>
int main() {
    //This is used to define an octal literal
    int i=0313;
    //This is used to define a hexadecimal literal
    int i1=0x3c;
    std::cout << "The value of the octal literal is " << i <<
std::endl;
    std::cout << "The value of the hexadecimal literal is " << i1
<< std::endl;
    return 0;
}
```

With this program, the output is as follows:

The value of the unsigned integer literal is 203

The value of the long integer literal is 60

Floating point literals

A floating-point literal has an integer part, a decimal point, a fractional part, and an exponent part. The floating-point literals can be represented either in decimal form or exponential form.

The following program is used to showcase the use of floating-point literals.

```cpp
#include <iostream>
int main() {
    //This is used to define a floating point literal with a decimal point
    float f=3.14;
    //This is used to define a floating point literal with an exponential point
    float f2=314567E2;
    std::cout << "The value of the floating point literal with a decimal point is " << f << std::endl;
    std::cout << "The value of the floating point literal with an exponential point is " << f2 << std::endl;
    return 0;
}
```

With this program, the output is as follows:

The value of the floating point literal with a decimal point is 3.14

The value of the floating point literal with an exponential point is 3.14567e+007

Character literals

A character literal is enclosed within single quotes. Also in addition to defining normal characters you can also define escape sequences. So for example, if you wanted to have a new line character, you would define the character as /n.

Below is the table for the various escape sequences.

Escape sequences

Escape sequence	Meaning
\\	This defines the \ character
\'	This defines the ' character
\"	This defines the " character
\?	This defines the ? character
\a	This defines the alert or bell
\b	This defines the backspace character
\f	This defines the form feed character
\n	This defines the new line character
\r	This defines the carriage return character
\t	This defines the horizontal tab
\v	This defines the vertical tab

The following program is used to showcase character literals.

```cpp
#include <iostream>
int main() {
    //This is used to define a character literal
    char c='B';
    std::cout << "The value of the floating constant is " << c
<< std::endl;
    std::cout << "An example of the tab and new line escape
sequence\tis\nshown below";
    return 0;
}
```

With this program, the output is as follows:

The value of the floating constant is B

An example of the tab and new line escape sequence   is

shown below

String literals

String literals are nothing but a series of characters.

The following program is used to showcase string literals.

```cpp
#include <iostream>
int main() {
    std::cout << "An example of a string literal \tis\nshown
below";
    return 0;
}
```

Chapter 10 : Signed and Unsigned Data types

For some of the data types, such as the char and integer you have a further classification:

• One is the breaking of an integer into a short and long integer.

• And next is the ability to add signs for a value to indicate whether it is a signed or unsigned value.

Data types ranges for short, long, signed and unsigned

Type	Range
char	-128 to 127 or 0 to 255
unsigned char	0 to 255
signed char	-128 to 127
int	-2147483648 to 2147483647
unsigned int	0 to 4294967295
signed int	-2147483648 to 2147483647
short int	-32768 to 32767
unsigned short int	0 to 65,535
signed short int	-32768 to 32767
long int	-9,223,372,036,854,775,808 to 9,223,372,036,854,775,807
signed long int	-9,223,372,036,854,775,808 to 9,223,372,036,854,775,807
unsigned long int	0 to 18,446,744,073,709,551,615
float	+/- 3.4e +/- 38
double	+/- 1.7e +/- 308

The following program is used to showcase the way we can define unsigned and signed values in C++.

```cpp
#include <iostream>
int main() {
    unsigned char c1=244;
    signed char c2=-100;
    unsigned int i1=1;
    signed int i2=-11;
std::cout << "An example of an unsigned character value is " << int(c1) << std::endl;
std::cout << "An example of a signed character value is " << int(c2) << std::endl;
std::cout << "An example of an unsigned integer value is " << i1 << std::endl;
std::cout << "An example of a signed integer value is " << i2 << std::endl;
    return 0;
}
```

With this program, the output is as follows:

An example of an unsigned character value is 244

An example of a signed character value is -100

An example of an unsigned integer value is 1

An example of a signed integer value is -11

The following program is used to showcase the way we can use short and long integers in a C++ program.

```cpp
#include <iostream>
int main() {
    short int i1=1;
    long int i2=110000000;
    std::cout << "An example of a short integer value is " <<
int(i1) << std::endl;
    std::cout << "An example of a long integer value is " <<
int(i2) << std::endl;
    return 0;
}
```

Chapter 11 : Introduction to Classes

At the heart of all object-oriented programming lies the notion of classes, objects that you create and utilize all throughout your code. This helps with modularity, with ease of use, with efficiency, and with higher-level programming that is far more logical and coherent.

In the early iterations of C, there was a primitive sort of class called a struct. Structs still exist in C++ but are mainly deprecated and shirked in favor of using classes instead. Nevertheless, structs are important to cover. C++ structs are also different from C structs. C structs didn't have much of the functionality which C++ structs do.

Before we jump into that, let's talk briefly about the notion of access modifiers.

We've talked about things like *int, string, bool,* and *float,* called types. We created what could be considered somewhat of a type using enumerators. However, you can create an entire type that is made up of smaller pieces of data and innate functions. This is called an object.

Access modifiers describe what is able to change what within your code. There are three different access modifiers.

Public access means that the object and/or its internal data and functions can be accessed and modified by any other code in the program.

Protected means that the object and/or its internal data and functions can be access and modified by only its derivatives. (This will make sense when we get into inheritance and polymorphism.)

Private means that only the object itself can access and modify its data.

This is important for purposes of security, clarity, and code safety.

Structs and classes are both ways to create new objects. The primary difference between structs is that structs are public by default and classes are private by default. Other than that, the differences are very negligible.

However, in the tech industry, structs have a fair bit of a negative connotation. Developers tend to see them as unprotected objects with little functionality, while they tend to see classes as very functional objects with child classes that are well made and well structured.

As such, it's generally better to create classes unless your object has very little in the way of functionality and simply contains very little data and innate function.

Look at this struct and declaration.

```
struct animal {

    enum diet { herbivore, omnivore, carnivore };

    int legs;

    string name;

    diet naturalDiet;

};

int main() {

    animal dog;

    dog.legs = 4;
```

dog.name = "Dog";

dog.naturalDiet = dog.carnivore;

This is the absolutely most simple way to declare a new object. You should absolutely not declare them within an existent function.

Let's go ahead and replace that struct with a class, because we're going to be using classes going forward as they're generally a safer and better option than structs are.

Create a new project in CodeBlocks called "AnimalSimulator". Not the most creative title, but it'll absolutely work for what we've got to do. Redact the contents of main.cpp and import iostream and create your main method.

Above the main method, let's declare a class called Animal. You would do that very similarly to how you'd declare a struct. For the sake of illustration, make it look like this:

```
class animal {

    string name;

};
```

Then within your main method, declare an instance and set its instance of name to the name of your favorite animal. Afterward, try to build.

You should have gotten an error that said "error: string animal::name is private".

Perfect. This is absolutely supposed to happen, because now we have to fix this. This is where that whole notion of access description comes in.

Modify your class so that it looks like this:

```
class animal {

    public:

        string name;

}
```

Then try to build. It should work fine this time. That's because we made the string "name" public, which means other methods/functions outside of the class itself can access it.

This is generally considered bad practice though, so we're going to rewrite the class like so:

```
class animal {

    private:

        string name;

}
```

The best-practice way to modify values within a class is to use get/set methods. Here's the way the class would look if you implemented get/set methods.

```
class animal {

    private:
```

```
        string name;

    public:

        string getName() {

            return this->name;

        }

        void setName(string name) {

            this->name = name;

        }

    }
```

Now, in your main method, after declaring whatever animal it is, instead of directly modifying its name, you should instead use the get/set method like so (assuming your instance animal is called "dog"):

dog.setName("dog");

Then you can test this by printing out the name in your main method:

cout << "The name of my favorite animal is: " << dog.getName() << "\n";

The way these work is by returning or setting the value of the variable via a method from within the class. "this->" is called the *this pointer*, and it refers to the variable of a given instance of a class. Every object has access to its own variables and can modify them directly via the 'this pointer'.

Anyway, your code should work stunningly. But what if you don't want to go through get/set for every instance of every class? Well, you use what's called an initializer function.

Modify your class so it looks like this:

```
class animal {
        private:
                string name;
        public:
                animal(string name) {
                        this->name = name;
                }
                string getName() {
                        return this->name;
                }
                void setName(string name) {
                        this->name = name;
                }
        }
```

Now, in your main function, take out the chunk of code that says *animal x* followed by the *x.setName("name")* function. When you create an initializer function, you can set certain variables from the get-go.

For example, since your initializer function takes the argument of *name*, you can declare that when you declare the variable and circumvent the whole setName operation. Look at this code for an example:

animal dog("dog");

animal elephant("elephant");

animal bird("bird");

These are all separate instances of the class animal, and their names have been set without the use of a set function thanks to the function initializer.

This can take as many arguments as you'd like it to. This makes it incredibly easy to create new objects and pretty streamlined of a process too.

Now that we've spoken for a moment about declaring objects and things of that nature, let's talk more about the specifics of what you can do with them. The object *animal* here, represents, of course, animals. We can give the entire class a set of methods that they can perform.

Let's think for a second about what every animal does. Every animal sleeps, eats, and drinks, right? So it wouldn't be very outlandish to include these within our class so that every member object of the class animal is able to perform these methods.

Let's say we had two specific kinds of food: meat, and plants, both of which also represented by their own respective objects.

We could create two different functions for this:

```
void eat(plant p) {

        // code here

}
void eat(meat m) {

        // code here

}
```

Even though these share a name, you can call either depending upon the type of object which you put include in the function call, and both will perform their respective code in response to the argument which you included. This is called *function overloading*. It's an essential technique in object-oriented programming that will help you to create functional and clear sets of code that are easy for people to use and understand.

Because it's unwieldy to create a large number of types while we're learning about classes in the first place, let's just leave "eat" as a void function which doesn't take arguments. Your code should look like this:

```
class animal {

        private:
```

```
        string name;
public:
        animal(string name) {
                this->name = name;
        }
        string getName() {
                return this->name;
        }
        void setName(string name) {
                this->name = name;
        }
        void eat() {
                // eat food
        }
}
```

Chapter 12 : Deeper Class Concepts

When C++ was being designed by AT&T engineer Bjarne Stroustrup as a language which would extend C, it was actually called *C with Classes* at first. Resultantly, one can make the not-so-bold assumption that C has a wealth of things which you can do with classes. This assumption would be 100% correct. Classes have several different functionalities built in that make them a joy to work with.

The first we should consider is called *inheritance*. This is a concept which allows a class to draw from a parent class. Let's go back to the animal class.

Because all dogs are animals, we can create a derivative of the animal class to represent dogs.

In order to inherit it, we'd have to do the following:

```
class dog : public animal {

    // code goes here

};
```

Now, let's try to change some things around. First, above your string constructor function in the *animal* class, create a constructor which doesn't take arguments and sets this->name to a blank string.

```
animal() {

    this->name = "";
```

}

Then go back to the dog class and create a mimic constructor, but here, set this->name equal to "dog". Don't forget to make your constructor public.

```
dog() {

        this->name = "dog";

}
```

Perfect. Technically, this is exactly what I've asked you to do. However, if you try to compile that, it doesn't work. You get the heads up that "string animal::name" is private, and those can't be modified.

This means that back in our animal class code, we need to make this essential change:

```
class animal {

        private:

                string name;

[...]
```

needs to become

```
class animal {

        protected:

                string name;

[...]
```

This is because in order to access this variable from child objects, we have to set the access modifiers in the ultimate parent function for this variable to *protected*. Now, child classes can access and modify this variable, but any given function in the program otherwise cannot.

Because all dogs are animals but not all animals are dogs, we can define specific functions here that dogs will perform which other animals obviously won't.

Back in your dog class, create a function under the *public* access modifier which is called "bark".

```
public:

    void bark() {

        cout << "\nBark!\n"

    }
```

Now go to your main method and declare an instance of dog. For the sake of example, mine will be called "d". Afterward, create an instance of the animal class.

```
    Try to access bark() from both.

int main() {

    dog d;

    animal a;

    dog.bark();

    animal.bark();
```

```
        }
```

If you try to compile, you should get the error that "'class animal' has no member named 'bark'." Great! This is exactly what was supposed to happen. Because dog is a derived class from animal, you can define functions in it that a dog can use but something broadly defined as an animal cannot - for example, barking.

Remove a.bark(), then compile and launch. It should work perfectly.

But wait! I know what you're thinking. "There are types of dog too. And furthermore, not every dog *barks*, small dogs *yip*, genius." I'm well aware. Don't worry - we can derive classes from derived classes, too!

Below your dog class, add in a class called "smallDog" which is inherited from dog.

```
class smallDog : public dog {

        public:

        smallDog() {

                this->name = "small dog";

        }

};
```

Now if, in our main function, we create an instance of smallDog called sd, and try to declare bark after dog d barks, we'll have two barks on the screen. But you're right - small dogs *don't* bark. How do we go about fixing this?

This is where something called *function overriding* comes into play.

To override a function, you only need to rewrite it (unless it's a virtual function, in which case it needs the override specifier.)

In class *smallDog*:

void bark() {

    cout << "\nYip!\n";

Now, in your code, sd.bark() should produce "yip" while d.bark() produces "bark". This is the essential nature of function overriding in C++.

Function overriding is an integral part of the object-oriented concept known as "polymorphism". What this means is that things can have different meanings depending upon the context. Inheritance and polymorphism are two key concepts of object-oriented programming.

Another important concept is the notion of abstraction. Abstraction is the idea of keeping the user-level side of programming as error-free and easy to maintain as possible, often by providing functions for performing certain actions upon variables that are protected by the classes themselves from user-level access which could inadvertently cause harm to the overall program.

One more important object-oriented concept is the idea of encapsulation, which is a mechanism of putting data and functions which use them together. Classes innately offer encapsulation. Encapsulation and abstraction go hand in hand by hiding data that could potentially cause an error, instead offering methods by which to access, utilize, and manipulate the data.

Anyway, getting off of the broader concepts, it's very important to cover the topic of virtual functions.

It's a little difficult to explain why virtual functions are important, but I'm going to try, because they very much are.

The simplest way to explain it is this: let's say you've got two classes, a base class and a derived class. We can go back to the example of animals/dogs. Animals would eat generic food, while dogs would eat - of course - dog food.

If they both had a function called "isEating()" which would output what they were eating, the animal object would output "generic food" while the dog object would output "dog food". This is fine and all for the purpose of a main function, but it falls apart if they have to go through an intermediate function.

For example, if in the main function, there were a reference to another function called "makeAnimalsEat(animal &a)", and the referenced animal a were to call .isEating(), then all objects derived from the animal class would use the animal version of the function isEating and not their own overridden versions.

At first glance, a solution appears to overload the makeAnimalsEat(animal &a) function with another function that accepts specifically the derivative class *dog*, such as makeAnimalsEat(dog &d). But think about this a little further - there are a lot of animals in the world. A whole, whole lot. Are we really going to overload this same exact function repeatedly in order to make it work for every possible derivative of the animal class? Of course not, that's absurd.

The answer instead is to make the base class's isEating() function a virtual function, like so:

```
virtual void isEating() {

        cout << "generic food";

}
```

To override this function in derived classes, you type the override keyword after the function name, like this:

```
void isEating() override {

        cout << "dog food";

}
```

which would effectively solve the problem that had existed in the first place.

The last major concept of classes to cover (at least for the scope of this book) is the notion of *operator overloading*. There's a very simple way to describe this.

Think about if you had two integers a, 5, and b, 3. The equation:

a + b

would thus come out to 8. Right? This is because they have explicit values.

However, what if we had two members of a class called cube, and this class had length, height, and width as its properties.

If you had two cube objects named a and b and then tried to add them, there's no innate meaning to it. The compiler doesn't know how or in what way to add these two objects.

Create a new project called operatorOverloading and delete the contents of main.cpp. Create your main method and then create a cube class. It should have private variables length, height, and width, and public methods which set those values and return the volume (length * width * height), as well as a class constructor + an empty constructor.

Your code should end up looking a bit like this:

```
class cube {
    public:
        int getV() {
            return length * width * height;
        }
        void setL() {
        }
        void setW() {
        }
        void setH() {
        }
        cube() {
            this->length = 0;
            this->width = 0;
            this->height = 0;
        }
        cube(int length, int width, int height) {
            this->length = length;
```

this->width = width;

this->height = height;

 private:

  int length, width, height;

So with that done, we now need to look at how we could add two cube objects together.

Fortunately, you can actually overload the existent mathematical operators in C++ to give them new functions for your classes.

Here's how we would do such in this case.

First, in the public section of your cube code, you would act like you were making a constructor by declaring the object itself.

cube

Then you use the operator keyword and what specify which operator you want to override - in this case, the addition operator, followed by parameter parentheses and function brackets.

cube operator+(cube &add) {

Since we're passing through another object, we need to actually pass in the secondary variable's reference address. What's happening in this line of code is that you're overriding the addition operator, +, and specifying what happens when the object *cube* is combined with the operator and the object within the parameters. So basically, what happens when *this* instance of cube cube is added to another cube, here called *add*? Within the brackets, we need to specify what's going on.

In the brackets, we need to declare cube c.

Now, we need to say that cube c's length is equal to the length of the first cube instance (this->) plus the second cube instance defined in the function parameters (add).

c.length = this->length + add.length;

Then we do the same for the width and height.

By the end, your code should ideally look something along these lines:

```
cube operator+(cube &add) {

        cube c;

        c.length = this->length + add.length;

        c.width = this->width + add.width;

        c.height = this->height + add.height;

        return c;
```

If you wanted your code to be extra secure, you could actually make the variable within the parameters a constant.

```
cube operator+(const cube &add) {
```

Now we're going to talk about splitting your code up to make it incredibly readable and easier to use.

Chapter 13 : Object Oriented Programming

Objects and Classes

What makes C++ different from C is the addition of *object-oriented programming* (*OOP*). In OOP, programs are divided into objects, data structures that package the data and the functions that work with that data together.

In top-down design, your program is a set of functions, with the main function driving the whole program. In contrast, in object-oriented design, you first think about the data (the variables) in your problem, and then package up the data with the functions that use that data into objects.

To create an object, first you need to write a *class* which a data structure that holds both data and functions in it. When you design a class, you create a new data type. For example, you may write a class called Student that contains all the data about students like their name, id, gpa, etc. and then functions that let you input, output, and change this data. Then, you declare *object* variables that are of this new data type. For example, you can declare student1, student2, student3, or a whole array of student objects that are all of type Student.

There are 3 steps to writing an object-oriented program:

1.   Decide on the *shared data variables* (also called *member* or *instance variables*) and declare these variables as private in the class (they cannot be accessed outside of the class).

2.   Write the public functions that work with the shared variables inside the class.

3.   Write a main function that creates object(s) of that class and tests the functions. .

Here's how to write a new class called Student in C++:

class Student

private: // the data *(called* member *or* instance *or* shared variables*)*

string name;

long int id;

double gpa;

public: // the member functions

void inputData()

cout << "Please enter the student's name: ";

cin >> name; // has access to the shared variables above

cout << "Please enter the student's id: ";

cin >> id;

}

void calculateGPA()

{ ....}

}; // note the ; that ends the class definition

Then, you can write a main function that tests the new class by creating 3 Student objects s1, s2, s3, and call their public functions by using the . operator (which can be pronounced as 's, e.g. s1's inputData() function which will fill in s1's data):

int main()

Student s1, s2, s3;

s1.inputData();

s2.inputData();

s1.calculateGPA();

Object-Oriented Programming also follows the principle of *Data Encapsulation and Information Hiding.* It protects the data by making it private and provides public functions to securely access the data. The *private* specifier means that member variables are only accessible inside the class – they are shared and accessible by the functions inside that class. All shared variables in the class should be declared under private. The *public* specifier means that it is accessible by anyone anywhere (inside and outside the class). Functions are usually made public.

Most modern programming languages are now object-oriented because there are certain advantages to this type of programming. Here are some advantages of OOP:

- It protects the data. No one but your functions inside the class can change them.
- Functions tend to be shorter and better designed. Because they all share the private data variables, they have fewer arguments.
- Programmers make less errors because they don't have to pass around the data variables as arguments to functions.

- It's easier to extend a class and create a new class promoting *Software Reuse/ Inheritance.*

Member Functions inside a Class

Most classes have some standard functions written inside them:

- *Accessor/Mutator (get/set) functions*: simple functions called set and get that set a shared variable to a value and return (get) a shared variable.
- *Input/Output functions:* asks the user for the values for the shared variables or prints them out.
- *Constructor Functions:* initializes the shared variables.
- *Other Special Functions* (for example, deposit/withdraw for BankAccount class).

For example, here is the Student class again with get/set functions for the name of the student:

```
class Student

{

private:

string name;

long int id;

public:

void setName( string n )

name = n;

string getName()

return name;

void inputData()
```

```
cout << "Please enter the student's name: ";

cin >> name;

cout << "Please enter the student's id: ";

cin >> id;

void outputData()

cout << name << endl;

cout << id << endl;

}; // end of class
```

A special type of function in OOP is the *constructor function* which initializes all the shared variables to initial values. Constructor functions must have the same name as the class and no return type. They get called automatically when you create objects of the class. Here is a default constructor function Student() which gets called automatically when you declare an object of the class Student: e.g. Student s1;

```
Student()

name = ""; // initializes all the shared variables to default values

id = 0;

gpa = 0;
```

Constructors can also take arguments that are copied into the member variables:

```
public Student(String n, long int i) {
```

```
name = n;

int = i;

}
```

// Called in main() as: Student s1("Chris", 12345);

The keyword *this* is sometimes used inside the member functions to refer to the calling object, e.g. s1. So when we use name in the Student constructor above, we want this object, s1's, name, and could write this.name.

Programmers often divide up object-oriented programs into different files. The class definition with just the prototypes of the function goes into a header file, e.g. Student.h. The member functions are put in a different file, e.g. student.cpp, which includes the header file at the top, e.g. #include "Student.h". The main function is put in a separate file too, e.g. driver.cpp, and it includes the header file too. These files are all put into the same project (New/Project) in the editor and compiled together.

Array of Objects

Objects are often put into arrays or more complex data structures such as vectors. For example, we usually want more than a couple student objects in our programs. We might want to keep track of all the students in a classroom or even a school and need hundreds or thousands of students. The new class types we have created can be used everywhere a simple data type is used. So we can declare an array of Student objects as easily as declaring an array of ints:

Student studentArray[100]; // contains 100 Student objects

Or we can declare a dynamic array of students:

Vector students<Student>;

We can use loops to go through our array and call each student's functions:

for(int i=0; i < 100; i++)

studentArray[i].inputData(); // call student i's inputData() function

We can also pass the whole array to a function. For example,

void inputArray(Student studentArrayarray[ ]) {

for(int i=0; i < 100; i++)

studentArray[i].inputData();

Luckily, the array name always serves as its address in C++, so the array's address will be passed in automatically to the function, instead of copying the whole array, and will change the original array.

Projects

1.   Create a Date class that contains month, day, and year and set/get and input/output functions and a default constructor that sets the date to the current date. Test it out in a main function.

2.   Create a BankAccount class that contains information about a bank account (the owner, the balance, etc.) and the standard functions as well as functions to withdraw() and deposit().

3.   Create an Array of Student objects and use a loop to fill them with data. Then, find the student with the highest gpa.

Chapter 14 : Improved Techniques

Structures

Structs originate from C, and come from the world of pre-class programming. However, they're still useful and can be use in places where classes are deemed as overkill.

A good example of using a structure being used can be for record keeping, for example you needed to keep track of football players in a team you would need to store:

- Name
- Kit Number
- Wage
- Strongest foot
- Etc

If there is no need to add functionality onto this information a structure is perfect for this situation. A structure storing this information is defined like this:

struct **FootballPlayer**

{

string Name;

int KitNumber;

double Wage;

string StrongestFoot;

};

This structure contains all the values that are relevant, this will provide a relevant container for similar information.

A new instance of the structure is defined like so:

FootballPlayer player1;

player1.Name = "Messi";

player1.KitNumber = 10;

player1.Wage = 1000000;

player1.StrongestFoot = "Both";

This code will create a FootballPlayer and assign values to all its member variables.

Real world usage of structures tend to be "simple" usage where they need to just store trivial data like the example above, when there needs to be functionality and encapsulation use a class. This is known a POD (Plain Old Data) encapsulation.

Note: The default access for structure variables is public while classes default to private.

Enums

Enums is short for Enumerated Type as has the role of a boolean but with unlimited user defined types, this can be used a flags for a situation like "HOME_SCREEN" or "SETTING_SCREEN".

An enum is defined like so:

```
enum CurrentScreen
{
HOME,
SETTINGS,
CONTACTS,
CALCULATOR
};
```

With each word in the brackets being a state the enum can be set as. A enum instance is created like so:

```
int main()
{
CurrentScreen phone1;
phone1 = HOME;
}
```

This code above makes a new enum and assigns it as "HOME". You can now use the enum to check what states it is, the example below will use a switch-case:

```
#include "stdafx.h"
#include <iostream>
using namespace std;
```

```cpp
enum CurrentScreen
{
HOME,
SETTINGS,
CONTACTS,
CALCULATOR
};
int main()
{
CurrentScreen phone1;
//Change me
phone1 = HOME;
switch (phone1)
{
case HOME:
cout << "You're on the home page" << endl;
break;
case SETTINGS:
cout << "You're on the settings page" << endl;
break;
case CONTACTS:
cout << "You're on the contacts page" << endl;
```

```
break;

case CALCULATOR:

cout << "You're on the calculator page" << endl;
break;

default:

break;

}

}
```

Output
>You're on the home page

This code shows you can use conditional structures along with an enum to easily create a nice branched structure. Mess around with the commented "Change me" enum definition and see how the output changes.

Unions

Unions are a data structures designed to provide efficient memory usages, they can contain as many member variables as it needs however it can only store data for a single variable at a time. So the entire structure only takes up memory for the biggest member variable.

These have to be used with caution because setting value of another member variable will remove data stored in another, so it is incredibly easy to lose important data.

A union is defined like so:

union **Example**

{

int i;

int x;

int y;

};

And an instance and value is created like so:

Example e;

e.i = 4;

To show how the size of the union works the program below works it through:

```
#include "stdafx.h"

#include <iostream>

using namespace std;

union Example

{

int i;

int x;

int y;

};
```

```cpp
int main()
{
    Example e;

    e.i = 4;

    cout << "Your int size is: " << sizeof(int) << " bytes" << endl;
    cout << "The union has 3 variables that should be a total of:  " <<
    sizeof(int) * 3 << " bytes" << endl;
    cout << "However, the union is " << sizeof(e) << " bytes" << endl;
}
```

Depending on your CPU architecture your output will be:

Ouput

>Your int size is: 4 bytes

>The union has 3 variables that should be a total of: 12 bytes
>*However, the union is 4 bytes*

As you can tell the union is only the size of a single integer, these structures can be used to efficiently use memory is there're situations where variables are idle and only one is needed.

Below is code that shows what happens to all the values when one is changed:

```cpp
#include "stdafx.h"

#include <iostream>

using namespace std;
```

```cpp
union Example
{
int i;
int x;
int y;
};
void Print_Union(Example e)
{
cout << "i: " << e.i << endl;
cout << "x: " << e.x << endl;
cout <<"y: " << e.y << endl;
}
int main()
{
Example e;
cout << "1" << endl;
e.i = 4;
Print_Union(e);
cout << "2" << endl;
e.y = 3;
Print_Union(e);
```

```
cout << "3" << endl;
e.x = 1;
Print_Union(e);
}
```

Ouput

> 1

> i: 4

> x: 4

> y: 4

> 2

> i: 3

> x: 3

> y: 3

> 3

> i: 1

> x: 1

> *y: 1*

As you can tell when you change one value, they all equal the same value, this is because all values share the same memory location and therefore when one changes they all change.

Variable argument lists

Variable argument lists allow for the possibly of endless parameters. Before we have come across functions with a static set amount of parameters (variables you can pass into a method) like:

int Add(int i, int y)

{

}

Has two parameters integer "i" and integer "y".

This is known as a Variadic Function or a function with unlimited arity (parameter number, so "Add" above has an arity of 2)

The variables are stored in a variable known as the va_list this works as any other variable but it just holds the list of variables passed. A variadic function is defined like so:

void Add(int numberOfVariables, ...)

{

}

Where "numberOfVariables" is the number of extra parameters passed, note this does not include this variable. This is required because the va_list does not know the total number of variables and does not keep track of where it is in the list.

Using the va_ist requires the use of a few functions:

- *va_start*(va_list, numberOfVariables)

o **Grabs the variables passed in and assigns the number specified by the second parameter to the first parameter**

- *va_arg*(va_list, type)

o **Grabs the next variable from the specified list in the first parameter and creates a variable specified by "type"**

- *va_end*(va_list)

o **Tidies up the list specified**

We can now use these functions to create a working variadic function:

```
#include "stdafx.h"

#include <cstdarg>

#include <iostream>

using namespace std;

void Add(int numberOfVariables, ...)

{

//The variable list
```

```cpp
va_list arg;

//Grabs the list
va_start(arg, numberOfVariables);

int total = 0;

for (int i = 0; i < numberOfVariables; i++)

{

//Grabs the next variable
total += va_arg(arg, int);

}

//Clean up
va_end(arg);

cout << "Total is: " << total << endl;

}

int main()

{

//4 Arguments
Add(4,

1, 2, 3, 4);

//10 Arguments
Add(10,

6, 9, 5, 11, 22, 1, 3, 56, 90, 63);

}
```

Ouput

>Total is: 10

>*Total is: 266*

Each section of the variable list process is labelled, this function adds all parameters it's given. This gives a very dynamic way to create one function that can handle an almost infinite list of parameters.

Exercise

Create a function that multiplies all the parameters given and returns a value, print out that value. Note: this #include is required:

#include <cstdarg>

Solution

Something like this:

```
#include "stdafx.h"

#include <cstdarg>

#include <iostream>

using namespace std;

int Multi(int numberOfVariables, ...)

{

va_list arg;

va_start(arg, numberOfVariables);
```

```cpp
int total = 1;

for (int i = 0; i < numberOfVariables; i++)

{

//Grabs the next variable
total *= va_arg(arg, int);

}

va_end(arg);

return total;

}

int main()

{

cout << "The total is: " << Multi(3, 56, 90, 63) << endl;

}
```

Namespaces

Namespaces are used to prevent variables and functions with the same name getting mixed up, for example the function Run() can be applicable in many situations so there needs to be a way to distinguish between different Run() functions, this is where namespaces can be used.

They are defined like so with all functions and variables in the curly brackets being part of that namespace:

```cpp
namespace NamespaceName
{

}
```

The example below shows how they are used:

Two namespaces are defined like so with the same function name:

```cpp
namespace Proccesing
{
void Run()
{
cout << "Processing!" << endl;
}
}
namespace Initialisation
{
void Run()
{
cout << "Initialisation started!" << endl;
}
}
```

This gives the programmer the opportunity to pick which Run() they can execute by just specifying the namespace like so:

```
    Proccesing::Run();
```
and

```
    Initialisation::Run();
```
and with them both run together:

```
int main()

{

Initialisation::Run();

Proccesing::Run();

}
```

Output

> Initialisation started!
> *Processing!*

Namespaces therefore gives a way to neatly segment code, and improves readability by providing a way to almost label blocks of code.

1.   What is the recommended situation you should use a struct?

2.   What is enum short for?

3.   How the size of a union dictated?

4.   What is a key factor about a union?

5.   What is a Variadic function?

6.   What does a va_list hold?

7.   Why do you need to specified the number of parameters in a variable function?

8.   Why does va_end() need to be run?

9.   What is the base role of a namespace?

10.   What syntax is used when calling a function inside a namespace, say you're calling the function Add() inside the namespace Math?

Answers

1.   For plain old data (POD).

2.   Enumerated type.

3.   It's the size of its largest member variable

4.   All the member variables share the same memory location so only on variable can hold a value at once

5.   A function with a possibly unlimited number of parameters

6.   A list of passed in variables to a function

7.   There is no way to tell the size of a va_list, so you need to specify the number of passed parameters

8.   It performs the clean-up of the variable list when it has been used

9.   To segment and label variables and functions in a meaningful way.

10.   Math::Add()

Chapter 15 : Multithreaded Applications in C++

If you are a pro in C++ programming or you have been building software for the past five years, chances are that you know Win32 threads. One of the greatest challenges that you have experienced when you create cross-platform software using C++ has been about threading in the right way. Since a lot of systems have different methods of multithreading, your source code can get muddy with all different kinds of preprocessor conditions that define the behavior of each platform. C++ has something called *std::thread*

The good thing is that any C++ compiler can implement this thread. So if you are being pressured to use Dev-C++, then it is high time you should consider something else. Let's assume now that you have a compiler that will help you instead of dragging you behind. The best way to write the threaded software in C++ language is by using API.

It is not right to throw some lines of code at you and let you alone digest the rest.

So what are threads?

There are a lot of resources online that talk about threads and it is good to read some of them. Let's get back to the main issue. Threads support software so that it can run in different processors simultaneously and in parallel. Well, it sounds good, right?

Although it is something good, still it comes with some problems. This makes it hard to think about performance when you don't have a well-defined design.

If you are still not okay with what threads are and why they are that useful, then you should take time and read some brief articles about threads.

Consume, Produce

One of the most popular examples of multithreading is the producer-consumer example. In other words, there is one thread which releases values for one to compute and the other thread receives the values to use it. This is a normal description that anyone can figure out.

In this example, you will realize that there are three related thread constructs. The three threads are explained below:

- *std::mutex*

This represents a single mutex. It is an object that gives access to a single thread in a given section.

- *std::lock_guard*

This locks a mutex that is in the scope. Once it is out of scope it is removed.

- *std::thread*

This displays a single thread executed.

The producer in this program increases the shared data object to 5 while the main thread increases the data object until the 5 is defined by the producer thread.

The most interesting thing is the way in which it is easy to create a thread, most specifically when you want to initialize a *std::thread*. What is done is to provide a function for the thread to implement plus its function arguments. In addition, the global mutex* helps protect data from multiple modifications. Lastly, use {...} to define explicit scopes while *std::lock_guard* should control access.

Two Tasks: One Process

What if you are writing software that is parallel? The example used requires one to build a distinct function in parallel for two separate values. This is the best case to use a Future object to complete the asynchronous computation.

A future is an object that ensures the right value exists depending on the type of computation. This object resembles a placeholder value. It helps a programmer to start a computation and confirm a result that has been produced.

To be precise, asynchronous result develops future objects. The std::promise, std::async, and std::packaged represent the interfaces that allow the implementation of a get_future() method.

- *Std::async*

This is an advanced method which provides a value for the future and creates the least flexibility. Besides that, it is the easiest way to implement asynchronous computation. You need to remember that this method does not resemble other objects.

- *Std::promise*

It presents a value to the future.

- *Std::packaged_tasks*

It is among the best ways one can deliver a future value.

Chapter 16 : War with bugs

It is very frustrating to spend more time searching for and removing bugs than writing your C++ programs. Therefore, the following suggestions can help you reduce the errors and make programming a great experience.

Develop a clear and consistent style of coding

By choosing to write C++ programs in a way that is consistent and clear not only improves the ease of another programmer going through your program but it also reduces coding mistakes.

Therefore, when you read a neat and clear code that follows a given style, you will spend a little amount of time to parse the syntax of the C++ statements. This leaves you with a lot of energy to decide what your program is going to do and how it is going to do it. A proper coding style should have the following characteristics:

1.   *Understand how the function, class, and object are used depending on their name.*

2.   *Distinguish between object names, function names, and class names.*

3.   *Distinguish between preprocessor symbols from the C++ symbols.*

4.   *Search the same level for blocks of code.*

Besides this, you must develop a standard format for your module headers and supply information related to classes, functions, author-date, and something about the history of modification.

Tip

All programmers working on a solo project should use the same coding style. Programs written in different coding styles confuse and sound unprofessional.

Turn on Warning and Error Messages

The syntax of C++ language provides the ability to check errors. Anytime a compiler comes across a construct that is difficult to decipher, it has nothing else to do but to display a message. It attempts to sync and back up the source code. There are times when this process is successful but it will not create an executable file. This will force the programmer to deal with all the error messages.

Nonetheless, once a C++ program finds a structure which it can run but the structure looks fishy, it will simply send a warning message. And the reason for this is because C++ language knows exactly what you want, so it proceeds and builds an executable file that will help you ignore the warnings. However, if you don't want to be disturbed, you can deactivate the warnings.

Tip

Disabling warnings is a really bad idea. It is like disconnecting the check engine in the car. Remember. Ignoring a problem is not a solution.

Comment on the Code

Errors can be prevented when one comments on the code. Make it a habit to comment your code when you write instead of waiting until when things work then you can return to comment. Comments are a great way to help you understand what you are trying to do. Short comments are better when you revise your program.

Limited Visibility

Reducing the accessibility to the external world of the inner members of a class is a key part in object-oriented programming. The class has to be accounted for its members. If something goes wrong in the class, then it is the fault of the programmer.

Limited visibility calls for data members to protect accessibility beyond the class. In short, the data members should be protected. Also, all member functions which the application software should not be aware of must be protected.

Monitor the heap memory

Forgetting to monitor the heap memory is one of the major sources of fatal errors in many released programs. This is again one of the hardest problems for one to track since this particular class of error is difficult to locate and remove. Most of the time, it exists in programs you buy. It will require you to run the program for many hours before problems start to show up. Programmers need to allocate and release a heap of memory as a general rule.

Use Exceptions to fix errors

To handle errors in the C++ language, the exception mechanism is built. Generally, it is good to send an error indicator instead of a return error flag.

Tip

Use exceptions to errors that are true. It is irrelevant to throw an exception from a function which sends an indicator that something didn't work.

Remove pointers once you delete what they point to

Ensure that you remove pointers once you delete what they were pointing to. You do this by allocating the pointers a nullptr value. You will come to learn about this in time. You may easily find yourself using a memory block returned to the heap when you don't know. There is a chance for a program to run well 99 percent of the time, but it would be hard to identify the 1 percent of instances when the block is assigned and the program fails to work.

In case you null out false pointers and try to use them to store a value, your program will immediately crash. A program crash is a bad thing, but it also reveals a problem. The problem exists, it is just a question of whether you can find it or not.

Declaration of virtual destructors

Make sure that you define a destructor in your class when a constructor allocates resources that should be returned when the object ends. Make the destructor visual once you have defined it.

Copy constructor and overloaded assignment operator

If your class will need a destructor, it really needs an overloaded assignment operator plus a copy constructor. If your constructor assigns resources such as the heap memory, the assignment operator and default copy constructor will not perform anything to create problems through producing multiple pointers.

If one destructor for these objects is invoked, it will return the assets. And when the destructor for the other copy appears, it spoils up things.

Follow every step in the debugger

Being a programmer, it is your role to understand whatever your program is doing. It is not enough that the program displays the required value. You must understand everything that your program does. There is no better way to understand what your program is doing than following up step by step. Get a good debugger and execute your program stepwise.

Again, while you debug your program, have with you some raw data to help you figure out any strange behavior that may arise when your program runs. There is no better way to do a complete check than monitoring each function as it runs.

Once a function ends and you need to add it to the program, you need to track the logical path at least once. When you review a function independently, bugs can be identified much easier rather than in a collection of other functions.

Chapter 17 : The New Versions: C++ 14

C++ 14 was released in December of 2014. It was often coined "C++1y" up until it's release. C++14 added a plethora of updates to the core language. In many instances C++14 builds upon functionality which was added within C++11. Overall it is a much daintier version with less impact on users.

Return Type Deduction
C++11 brought about the onset of lambda expressions and allowed them to determine the return type based on the expression. This newer version gave this ability to all functions. The use of auto is needed in order to determine the return type.

Relaxed Restrictions constexpr

C++11 also brought about the notion of constexpr- declared function. This is essentially a function which can be execute at the time of compile. In C++11 a constexpr function could only have one expression.

C++14 decreased the amount of restrictions which were present in version 11. These functions are now able to include the following:

- All declarations except thread_local or static variable types or any declarations without initialization

- Conditions including if statements and switches

- Any loop statements including for or while

The use of *goto* statements has been forbidden in this version of C++.

Number Separators

C++14 now gives users the option of using digit separators. This is simply a single quote used in numeric literals. This includes integers and floating integers.

The feature is anything but earth shattering however it is useful for the reading of numbers. The separator will not change the evaluation of the number and holds no particular coding advantage accept readability.

The sample below identifies how it is used.

Keyword: auto

The auto keyword is something new within C++14. Although it was previously introduced in C++3, it now has a different meaning. Its intention is to make coding easier, cleaner and prone to less mistakes. The following is an example of how auto can be used and its equivalent.

The above example is used instead of:

The use of auto also does not have any negative impact on speed. This is due to the fact that auto is deduced at the time of compile instead of the run time. Unlike with in C++11, auto can now be used with functions. You now have the ability to write:

Example Programs
The following are examples of the use of the keyword auto in C++11 and C++14.

1)   This is the C++11 version of a program.

The C++14 version is as follows:

Generic Lambdas

Lambda functions were introduced in C++11, where they needed to be declared as concrete types. C++14 is more lenient in its use of this requirement. It allows lambda parameter to be declared as a type of auto.

auto f = [](auto x){ return func(normalize(x)); };
The above given definition is equivalent to the following pseudo code:

The closure's function call operator is listed above.

In order to correctly write a lambda x must be perfectly forwarded to normalize. It must also be passed to the normalize via std::forward.

Find below a complete program example for the basic use of generalized lambdas.

The result of running the above code is as follows:

New Standard Library Features

With the onset of C++14 come new standard library features. These features include:

- Locking and shared mutexes

- Heterogeneous lookups within associative containers

- Standard literals defined by users

- Tuple addressing

This is a listing of the main library features that C++14 has to offer, there are also a vast amount of smaller library addition.

User Defined Literals

C++14 added a number of suffixes which are used to specify the type of defined literal. Some examples of these suffixes include 's' or 'st'. This is for the character and string type.

The last line of the given example will throw an error. This is because str will be determined as 'const char*' type however str1 will be determined to be a string.

The following suffixes – 'h', 'min', 's', 'ms', 'us', 'ns' are used to signify various time duration interval types.

Binary Literals

Up until the advent of C++14 binary literals like 11111101 were not supported. IN order to use them they needed to be converted to a supported type. The following code snippet shows how they are used in programming.

Binary laterals begin with ob or oB. This prefix is then followed by a series of zeros and ones. A similar syntax can be found in a variety of other programming languages. The programming languages include Java, Perl and Python, all of which already provide support for binary literals.

The binary literal has a type of int. It is accepted in all places that a constant literal is accepted.

Variable Template

The intended purpose of a variable template is to make coding easier and simplify definitions and the use of constants. A variable template essentially is the definition for a group of variables.

A variable template is created by using a template declaration at the place at which a variable is declared.

These are simply a few of the features which were introduced with C++14. A number of other features were introduced but are not strong advancements. Some of the minor features which were included with C++14 include sized deal locations and some syntax tidying. Although the C++14 versioning does not compare to the major updates in C++11 it is necessary.

Chapter 18 : Game Design

Introduction to Game Design

At this point, you know how to do many things in C++, and you've practically learned everything this book has to offer. This unit is dedicated solely to making computer games you could mess with when your internet is down. You won't learn much from this, but it is more of a way to gain experience.

These games pass time and are fun to play until the internet comes back. You will focus on games that are easy to make. Each time, the represented game will focus deeper on complex subjects and user relationships.

All of these upcoming games will be one player against the computer, so you don't have to worry about bringing a friend to play along with you.

However, you can modify the games to have a multiplayer mode, but it won't be a big requirement for a good basic stencil.

User Friendliness

User-friendliness is the term used when evaluating how easy it is to use your program. Even if you make a really complex program, the user should have a practical time using it. Confusing controls and limited ideals of input can confuse the user, and the user will not like your program, and you'll be sad because your program failed to succeed because no one liked it.

Here's just one example of making a program more user-friendly.

Say you have a program to display some even numbers, and here's what the program looks like when run.

Suppose someone saw that program. We can't assume that the user automatically knows that these are even numbers. A viable solution would be to say that these are even numbers.

Now that looks a tad nicer. This is a great way to spice up your programs so they look even cooler. The user now knows what is being displayed.

Remember to keep these messages simple and short. Don't make a long description, but know that the user needs to know what is happening.

Heads or Tails

This is the first game you will make. It will involve some basic skills that you will need to recover. Hopefully you haven't forgotten anything at this point.

Game Basis: A coin has two sides. It has a head and a tail. In a moment, the coin will be thrown in the air and will land on either heads or tails. Before it gets tossed, you have to guess whether the coin will land on either heads or tails. The coin gets tossed. If it lands on the side you guess, then you win the game. Otherwise you lose.

All of your real code will be implemented in the main method. However, feel free to put some of it in a function if you really want to.

Start with the logistics of what you need.

Since you need something to decide whether the coin will land on heads or tails, a random number generator works best because it generates random values, just as a coin flip will land on a random side.

Thus, include the Time and the Stdlib library at the top.

```
#include <iostream>
#include <time.h>
#include <stdlib.h>
using namespace std;
int main()
```

Now let's welcome the user with a greeting to let them know they are playing the game.

```
#include <iostream>
#include <time.h>
#include <conio.h>
#include <stdlib.h>
using namespace std;
int main()
{
    cout << "HEADS OR TAILS";
    cout << "\n\nPRESS ENTER TO CONTINUE...\n";
    cout << ">";
    getch();
```

"getch()" is a command to pause the program until the user presses 'Enter'. Above, you will need to include the Conio library (<conio.h>) because it holds the "getch()" command.

If otherwise, this is a decent way to start of a simple "text-based" game.

Now it is time for the real game. Ask the player if he or she chooses heads or tails, and let the user input the choice.

```
string choice;
cout << "\n\nI WILL FLIP A COIN.  DO YOU THINK IT WILL LAND ON HEADS OR TAILS?\n";
cin >> choice;
```

Now, decide whether the coin lands on either heads or tails. This is done with the random number generator. Even if numbers don't necessarily mean the actual sides on a coin. You can assign them yourself. In this case, the number 1 will be heads, and 2 will be tails.

So make a random number generator that will choose a number between 1 and 2. Quite the small range eh?

```
srand((unsigned)time(NULL));
int result = rand() % 2 + 1;
```

After flipping the coin, it's now time to decide the winner. This is done by telling different combinations of what the user picked and what the computer picked.

```
if (result == 1 && choice == "heads")
{
    cout << "\nYOU WIN!  IT LANDED ON HEADS!";
}
else if (result == 1 && choice == "tails")
{
    cout << "\nYOU LOSE.  IT LANDED ON HEADS.";
}
else if (result == 2 && choice == "heads")
{
    cout << "\nYOU LOSE.  IT LANDED ON TAILS.";
}
else
{
    cout << "\nYOU WIN.  IT LANDED ON TAILS!";
}
```

After that, you've sort of finished the whole game. Do note that you would have to enter your choice in lowercase the whole time, but feel free to edit the program to accept results with multiple cases like 'Heads', 'HEADS', or even 'hEads'.

Yes, cases like that can exist. You could even prepare for a event in which they spell the choice wrong.

Test it out and see what happens.

Full Program

```
#include <iostream>
#include <time.h>
#include <conio.h>
#include <stdlib.h>
using namespace std;
int main()
{
    cout << "HEADS OR TAILS";
    cout << "\n\nPRESS ENTER TO CONTINUE...\n";
    cout << ">";
    getch();
    string choice;
    cout << "\n\nI WILL FLIP A COIN.  DO YOU THINK IT WILL LAND ON HEADS OR TAILS?\n";
    cin >> choice;
    srand((unsigned)time(NULL));
    int result = rand() % 2 + 1;
    if (result == 1 && choice == "heads")
    {
        cout << "\nYOU WIN!  IT LANDED ON HEADS!";
    }
    else if (result == 1 && choice == "tails")
    {
        cout << "\nYOU LOSE.  IT LANDED ON HEADS.";
    }
    else if (result == 2 && choice == "heads")
    {
        cout << "\nYOU LOSE.  IT LANDED ON TAILS.";
    }
    else
    {
        cout << "\nYOU WIN.  IT LANDED ON TAILS!";
    }

}
```

Game Runthrough

Rock Paper Scissors

This will be very similar to the game you just made previously, but there are a few more complexities to it.

Game Basis: two players have one chance to choose among rock, paper, or scissors. At the same time, each player shows what he or she chooses using hand signals. The player's selection determines whether he or she wins or loses. For example, if player 1 chooses rock, and player 2 chooses scissors, player 1 will lose because rock's certain losing object is scissors, and scissors' certain winning object is rock. If both players choose the same object, the game ends in a tie. Below is a chart that demonstrates what object beats another.

As you see, you have an equal chance of winning, losing, or neither because you don't know what the other player will choose.

Start off with the basic outline you'll use for every game in this book, if you haven't realized. Now make your welcoming statement.

```
cout << "ROCK PAPER SCISSORS\n";
cout << "\nPRESS ENTER TO CONTINUE\n>";
getch();
```

Now, ask the player to choose between rock, paper, and scissors. In this version, the player can choose each choice based on the number they've been placed by, so if someone wanted to choose rock, he or she would have to insert 1, and etc.

```
cout << "\nROCK, PAPER, or SCISSORS (ENTER 1, 2, OR 3)";
cin >> choice;
```

Now let the computer choose its own choice. There is no actual way the player and the computer will choose the object at the same time, but even though the computer knows what you pick, it picks its object as though it has no idea of what you picked, and the choice will definitely not be based on what the player picked, just like in the heads or tails game.

Do note that it is possible to make the player lose, win, or tie all the time.

```
int compChoice = rand() % 3 + 1;
```

Now it's time to decide the winner of the game. The most simple algorithm to this strategy is to find the exact same combination of the two choices and printline the results out.

Once you start figuring it out, you'll soon realize it gets pretty long.

To make this as short as possible, first decide if there's a tie, which removes out the requirement of having to insert more conditional statements.

```
if (choice == compChoice)
{
    cout << "\nTIE, NO ONE WINS.";
}
```

The last step is to decide the winner if it's not a tie. Here is one of the most simplest ways you could do it, but it could take a while to get it all in. Oh well.

```
    else if (choice == 1 && compChoice == 2)
    {
        cout << "\nYOU LOSE. I CHOSE PAPER.  :)";
    }
    else if (choice == 1 && compChoice == 3)
    {
        cout << "\nYOU WIN!  I CHOSE SCISSORS.  :)";
    }
    else if (choice == 2 && compChoice == 1)
    {
        cout << "\nYOU WIN!  I CHOSE ROCK.  :)";
    }
    else if (choice == 2 && compChoice == 3)
    {
        cout << "\nYOU LOSE, I CHOSE SCISSORS.  :)";
    }
    else if (choice == 3 && compChoice == 1)
    {
        cout << "\nYOU LOSE. I CHOSE ROCK.  :)";
    }
    else
    {
        cout << "\nYOU WIN!  I CHOSE PAPER.  :)";
    }
```

You're sort of done at this point. Test it out, and see what happens.

Full Program

Game Runthrough

```
ROCK PAPER SCISSORS

PRESS ENTER TO CONTINUE
>
ROCK, PAPER, or SCISSORS (ENTER 1, 2, OR 3)3

YOU WIN!  I CHOSE PAPER.  :)
Process returned 0 (0x0)   execution time : 9.561 s
Press any key to continue.
```

If you thought that was hard, check the next one out.

161

Guess the Number

This is the final project you will do from this book.

Game Basis: One person will think of a random number from 1 - 100, and another has to guess that number in 10 tries. Each time the number isn't correct, they player will be told if it's higher or lower, and if the player fails to guess the number in 10 tries, he or she loses.

In this situation, you will have to guess a number the computer has chosen.

Start with your outline.

```
#include <iostream>
#include <time.h>
#include <conio.h>
#include <stdlib.h>
using namespace std;
int main()
{
    srand((unsigned)time(NULL));
}
```

Now have the computer create a number from 1 - 100.

```
int secretNum = rand() % 100 + 1;
```

Another way to start a good opening statement is with a plot, in which is used in this game.

```
cout << "GUESS THE NUMBER!!!\nPRESS ENTER TO CONITNUE.\n>";
getch();
cout << "\nI AM THINKING OF A NUMBER BEWTEEN 1 - 100 (SPOOKY).  DO YOU KNOW WHAT IT IS?\n";
```

Now let the user enter his or her first guess.

```
int guess;
cin >> guess;
```

Create the variable that will tell how many guesses the player has guessed. Right now, it starts at 0.

```
int c = 0; //c means count
```

In the game there will be some sort of loop. The loops will be repeating a set of commands to let the user try again until he or she runs out of tries. The commands will be detecting if the guess is higher, lower, or equal to the hidden number.

```
while (c < 10)
{

}
```

Whenever the execution goes to the start of the loop, there has been a new previous guess, so add 1 to count.

```
while (c < 10)
{
    c++; //c++ just like the language
}
```

Detecting whether the guess is higher, lower, or equal to the hidden number involves one big conditional which will detect the relationship between both numbers.

If the user guesses right, there is no need to use the loop, so the "break" statement will be used.

```
if (secretNum == guess)
{
    break;
}
```

If the user guesses higher or lower than the real number, tell the user to guess again, and whether it's too high or too low.

In review, this is what the loop looks like.

```
while (c < 10)
{
    if (secretNum == guess)
    {
        break;
    }
    else if (secretNum > guess)
    {
        cout << "\n\nTOO LOW.  GUESS AGAIN.\n>";
    }
    else
    {
        cout << "\n\nTOO HIGH.  GUESS AGAIN\n";
    }
    cin >> guess;
    c++;// just like the language
}
```

Now you get the loop, but what happens after that? If you look back at it, you'll see that the loop will only finish if the number is correct, or the player ran out of tries.

So you need to detect why the computer left the loop in order to tell if the player won by guessing the number, or lost by running out of tries.

Continue to make some more games and projects in C++. You are only limited by your imagination.

```
#include <iostream>
#include <time.h>
#include <conio.h>
#include <stdlib.h>
using namespace std;
int main()
{
    srand((unsigned)time(NULL));
    int secretNum = rand() % 100 + 1;
    cout << "GUESS THE NUMBER!!!\nPRESS ENTER TO CONTINUE.\n>";
    getch();
    cout << "\nI AM THINKING OF A NUMBER BEWTEEN 1 - 100 (SPOOKY).  DO YOU KNOW WHAT IT IS?\n";
    int guess;
    cin >> guess;
    int c = 0;
    while (c < 10)
    {
        if (secretNum == guess)
        {
            break;
        }
        else if (secretNum > guess)
        {
            cout << "\n\nTOO LOW.  GUESS AGAIN.\n>";
        }
        else
        {
            cout << "\n\nTOO HIGH.  GUESS AGAIN\n";
        }
        cin >> guess;
        c++;// just like the language
    }
    if (guess == secretNum)
    {
        cout << "\n\nYOU GUESSED THE CORRECT NUMBER! YOU WON IN " << c+1 << " TRIES!";
    }
    else
    {
        cout << "\n\nYOU FAILED TO GUESS THE NUMBER IN 10 TRIES. YOU LOSE.  THE NUMBER IS " << secretNum;
    }
}
```

Full Program Game Runthrough

Dragon Clash

Dragon Clash is a game made by the author. It's a text based battle game where two dragons, the Light Dragon and the Dark Dragon, take turns attacking each other or healing themselves until one of them has no more strength anymore.

It's not some 60 dollar hit at your local game store, but it should be fun to play. If this whole game took him several days to do, think of how long it took to create something that ended up inside a game store. Think of how many people it took to create something like that.

There is no official lesson on creating this. You will just be given the completed game.

```
#include <iostream>
#include <time.h>
#include <stdlib.h>
#include <conio.h>
using namespace std;
int main()
{
        srand((unsigned)time(NULL));
        int lightDragonHealth = 20;
        int darkDragonHealth = 20;
        bool win = false;
        int lightDragonCommand;
        cout << "000  000     0     000  00   0  0      000 0      0     00  0    0 0\n";
        cout << "0  0  0  0  0 0 0   0     0  0 00 0      0    0     0 0  0    0    0 0\n";
        cout << "0  0 000    000   0 00 0  0 00 0      0    0     000    00  00000 0\n";
        cout << "0  0  0  0 0   0   0 0  0 0 0 00      0    0     0  0    0 0    0  \n";
        cout << "000  0  0 0   00    00    00  0 00     000 0000 0   0  00  0    0 0\n\n";
        cout << "DARK DRAGON:     " << darkDragonHealth;
        cout << "\nLIGHT DRAGON:    " << lightDragonHealth;
        while (true)
        {
            cout << "WHAT WILL THE LIGHT DRAGON DO?\n";
```

```cpp
        cout << "COMMAND THE LIGHT DRAGON BY INPUTTING ITS ID NUMBER.\n\n";
        cout << "COMMAND NAME        STRENGTH                        ID NUMBER\n";
        cout << "BLUE FLAME BREATH   ATTACK 4 STRENGTH POINTS        1\n";
        cout << "CHARGE OF CHANCE    ATTACK 0 or 7 STRENGTH POINTS   2\n";
        cout << "ACCELERATED CARE    HEAL 5 STRENGTH POINTS          3\n";
        cout << ">";
        cin >> lightDragonCommand;
        if (lightDragonCommand == 1)
        {
            cout << "\nTHE LIGHT DRAGON UNLEASHED ITS BLUE FLAME BREATH\n";
            darkDragonHealth-=4;
            if (darkDragonHealth < 0)
            {
                darkDragonHealth = 0;
            }
            cout << "\nDARK DRAGON:  " << darkDragonHealth;
            cout << "\nLIGHT DRAGON:  " << lightDragonHealth << "\n\n";
            if (darkDragonHealth == 0)
            {
                win = true;
                break;
```

Full Program

```cpp
            }
        }
        else if (lightDragonCommand == 2)
        {
            cout << "THE LIGHT DRAGON IS USING ITS CHARGE OF CHANCE.\n";
            cout << "IT COULD EITHER STRIKE THE DRAK DRAGON HARSHLY, OR IT COULD MISS AND DO NOTHING.\n";
            int chargeChance = rand()%2 + 1;
            if (chargeChance == 1)
            {
                cout << "IT HITS!  THE DARK DRAGON HAS BEEN HURT BADLY.\n";
                darkDragonHealth -= 7;
                if (darkDragonHealth <= 0)
                {
                    darkDragonHealth = 0;
                    cout << "\nDARK DRAGON:  " << darkDragonHealth;
                    cout << "\nLIGHT DRAGON:  " << lightDragonHealth << "\n\n";
                    win = true;
                    break;
                }

            }

            else
            {
                cout << "UH OH, IT LOOKS LIKE IT MISSES AND THE DARK DRAGON HAS BEEN UNHARMED\n";
            }
            cout << "\nDARK DRAGON:  " << darkDragonHealth;
            cout << "\nLIGHT DRAGON:  " << lightDragonHealth << "\n\n";
        }
        else if (lightDragonCommand == 3)
        {
            cout << "THE LIGHT DRAGON IS USING ACCELERATED CARE.  IT WILL HEAL UP FOR A MOMENT OF TIME.\n";
            lightDragonHealth+=5;
            cout << "\nDARK DRAGON:  " << darkDragonHealth;
            cout << "\nLIGHT DRAGON:  " << lightDragonHealth << "\n\n";
        }
        cout << "IT LOOKS LIKE THE DARK DRAGON IS READY TO ATTACK.\n";
        int darkDragonCommand = rand()%3 + 1;
        if (darkDragonCommand == 1)
        {
            cout << "THE DARK DRAGON UNLEASHED ITS BLUE FLAME BREATH.\n\n";
            lightDragonHealth -= 4;
            if (lightDragonHealth < 0)
```

166

```cpp
        {
            lightDragonHealth = 0;
        }
        cout << "\nDARK DRAGON:   " << darkDragonHealth;
        cout << "\nLIGHT DRAGON: " << lightDragonHealth << "\n\n";
        if (lightDragonHealth == 0)
        {
            break;
        }
    }
    else if (darkDragonCommand == 2)
    {
        cout << "THE DARK DRAGON IS USING ITS CHARGE OF CHANCE.\n";
        cout << "IT COULD EITHER STRIKE THE LIGHT DRAGON HARSHLY, OR IT COULD MISS AND DO NOTHING.\n";
        int chargeChance = rand()%2 + 1;
        if (chargeChance == 1)
        {
            cout << "IT HITS!  THE LIGHT DRAGON HAS BEEN HURT BADLY.\n";
            lightDragonHealth -= 7;
            if (lightDragonHealth <= 0)
            {
                lightDragonHealth = 0;
                cout << "\nDARK DRAGON:   " << darkDragonHealth;
                cout << "\nLIGHT DRAGON: " << lightDragonHealth << "\n\n";
                break;
            }
        }
        else
        {
            cout << "IT LOOKS LIKE IT MISSES AND THE LIGHT DRAGON HAS BEEN UNHARMED";

        }
        cout << "\nDARK DRAGON:   " << darkDragonHealth;
        cout << "\nLIGHT DRAGON: " << lightDragonHealth << "\n\n";
    }
    else
    {
        cout << "THE DARK DRAGON IS USING ACCELERATED CARE.  IT WILL HEAL UP FOR A MOMENT OF TIME.";
        darkDragonHealth += 5;
        cout << "\nDARK DRAGON:   " << darkDragonHealth;
        cout << "\nLIGHT DRAGON: " << lightDragonHealth << "\n\n";
    }
}
if (win)
{
    cout << "CONGRATULATIONS, THE DARK DRAGON HAS BEEN DEFEATED!  YOU WON THE BATTLE!";
}
else
{
    cout << "THE LIGHT DRAGON HAS BEEN DEFEATED.  BETTER LUCK NEXT TIME.";
}
}
```

Game Runthrough

```
CHARGE OF CHANCE        ATTACK 0 or 7 STRENGTH POINTS      2
ACCELERATED CARE        HEAL 5 STRENGTH POINTS             3
>1

THE LIGHT DRAGON UNLEASHED ITS BLUE FLAME BREATH

DARK DRAGON:    13
LIGHT DRAGON:   17

IT LOOKS LIKE THE DARK DRAGON IS READY TO ATTACK.
THE DARK DRAGON IS USING ITS CHARGE OF CHANCE.
IT COULD EITHER STRIKE THE LIGHT DRAGON HARSHLY, OR IT COULD MISS AND DO NOTHING.
IT LOOKS LIKE IT MISSES AND THE LIGHT DRAGON HAS BEEN UNHARMED
DARK DRAGON:    13
LIGHT DRAGON:   17

WHAT WILL THE LIGHT DRAGON DO?
COMMAND THE LIGHT DRAGON BY INPUTTING ITS ID NUMBER.

COMMAND NAME            STRENGTH                           ID NUMBER
BLUE FLAME BREATH       ATTACK 4 STRENGTH POINTS           1
CHARGE OF CHANCE        ATTACK 0 or 7 STRENGTH POINTS      2
ACCELERATED CARE        HEAL 5 STRENGTH POINTS             3
>1

THE LIGHT DRAGON UNLEASHED ITS BLUE FLAME BREATH

DARK DRAGON:     9
LIGHT DRAGON:   17

IT LOOKS LIKE THE DARK DRAGON IS READY TO ATTACK.
THE DARK DRAGON UNLEASHED ITS BLUE FLAME BREATH.

DARK DRAGON:     9
LIGHT DRAGON:   13

WHAT WILL THE LIGHT DRAGON DO?
COMMAND THE LIGHT DRAGON BY INPUTTING ITS ID NUMBER.
```

```
COMMAND NAME            STRENGTH                           ID NUMBER
BLUE FLAME BREATH       ATTACK 4 STRENGTH POINTS           1
CHARGE OF CHANCE        ATTACK 0 or 7 STRENGTH POINTS      2
ACCELERATED CARE        HEAL 5 STRENGTH POINTS             3
>2
THE LIGHT DRAGON IS USING ITS CHARGE OF CHANCE.
IT COULD EITHER STRIKE THE DRAK DRAGON HARSHLY, OR IT COULD MISS AND DO NOTHING.
IT HITS!   THE DARK DRAGON HAS BEEN HURT BADLY.

DARK DRAGON:     2
LIGHT DRAGON:   13

IT LOOKS LIKE THE DARK DRAGON IS READY TO ATTACK.
THE DARK DRAGON UNLEASHED ITS BLUE FLAME BREATH.

DARK DRAGON:     2
LIGHT DRAGON:    9

WHAT WILL THE LIGHT DRAGON DO?
COMMAND THE LIGHT DRAGON BY INPUTTING ITS ID NUMBER.

COMMAND NAME            STRENGTH                           ID NUMBER
BLUE FLAME BREATH       ATTACK 4 STRENGTH POINTS           1
CHARGE OF CHANCE        ATTACK 0 or 7 STRENGTH POINTS      2
ACCELERATED CARE        HEAL 5 STRENGTH POINTS             3
>1

THE LIGHT DRAGON UNLEASHED ITS BLUE FLAME BREATH

DARK DRAGON:     0
LIGHT DRAGON:    9

CONGRATULATIONS, THE DARK DRAGON HAS BEEN DEFEATED!   YOU WON THE BATTLE!
Process returned 0 (0x0)   execution time : 18.276 s
Press any key to continue.
```

This game is over 100 lines long. You'll find many familiar subjects inside it. If you spend your time with it, you could find how your knowledge can be used to do such things.

Below is a link to the game's source in case you just want to copy and paste everything. You could understand how it works and even make it better. There are tons of ways to tweak it. This is just a small outline.

https://pastebin.com/TS8Zhffm

There is something that could bother a few. If you look closely, you'll see that there is a healing command. Your dragon can heal some of its health. However, there is no maximum amount of strength a dragon could have. It could run to an amount of hundreds of strength points. Try to fix that on your own and see if it works.

From this point you now have the ability to create many projects. This book is the beginning of your new computer science journey, taught by someone who is still beginning his also, considering his very young age at the time.

So this is the end of the book. Be sure to check out other tutorials to programming. There is way more to C++ than just what is in this book. Your journey to being a computer scientist has just begun.

Other Projects You Can Try

Game Link for Description Notes About the Game

Tic Tac Toe *http://www.wikihow.com/Play-TicTac-Toe*

Try to also add a bigger board (4x4, 5x5, 6x6, etc).

Hangman *http://www.wikihow.com/Play-Han gman*

Use a lot of words or phrases to add more interest.

Advance Nim *https://www.seeker.com/youre-alwa ys-a-winner-with-advance-nim-179 1396139.html*

Try to also make a different version where the computer is able to detect traps.

Secret Maze Challenge *https://en.wikipedia.org/wiki/Maze* Use Random to generate the outcome if you don't want to create an actual maze.

Scientific Calculator *https://en.wikipedia.org/wiki/Scient ific_calculator*

If you can, try to make a graphing calculator.

Adventure game using Dialog Tree *https://en.wikipedia.org/wiki/Dialog _tree*

Will need a lot of scenarios for best interest

Dictionary *https://www.vocabulary.com/dictio nary/dictionary*

Have the user enter a word and the computer will give a definition. You need to know what a hashmap is. After that, you'll find the algorithm quite simple, but you'll have to use a lot of words.

RPG https://en.wikipedia.org/wiki/Role-p laying_video_game

Will need a lot of scenarios for best interest, and doesn't have to be online

Prime   Number   Sequence *http://whatis.techtarget.com/definiti on/prime-number*

Prints the nth prime number in which n is an inputted number.

Fibonacci   Sequence   *https://en.wikipedia.org/wiki/Fibon acci_number*

Prints the nth fibonacci number in which n is an inputted number.

Binary Converter *https://www.mathsisfun.com/binary*

-number-system.html

You can also try ternary, quaternary, etc.

Midpoint Test (Answer Key)

Write the answer to each question clearly.

1. Name the mark used to end a statement.

a. ;

b. &

c. @

d. :

2. What is the difference between "cout" and "cin"?

cout outputs values, and cin lets the user enter values.

3. What kind of slash lets strings to become manipulated a little such as adding a new line to the string, or bringing a certain type of quote to it?

a. Forward Slash

b. Back Slash

4. Write down the symbol of division and modulus and explain the difference between their abilities (assume your values are integers).

Division displays the quotient and modulus displays the remainder.

5. What is the cause of a syntax error?

a. The computer has found something that it can't execute.

b. The computer can't read the script.

c. The computer has crashed.

d. The computer has a virus.

6. What is the difference between an float and a double? *A float holds less bytes than a double*

7. What is concatenation, and what symbol does it use? *The process of combining two strings. <<*

8. Write down the statement to include the time library. *#include <time.h>*

9. Assign 3 variables of 3 different types?

10. What is "include" used for? a. Erasing data

b. Calling libraries c. Calling methods d. Displaying values

11. Name 3 kinds of mathematical operations that can be done with the Math class. Answers vary. May include any of the following in this link

http://www.cplusplus.com/reference/cmath/

Chapter 19 Project: Agenda

For this project, we will simulate a phone agenda, like the one you have in your house and use them to keep record of all the important numbers you need, but we will do it using C++. For each contact, their name and their phone will be stored (although you can add as many fields as you want). Also, we will be using a new and very powerful feature of the Standard Template Library of C++: vector.

Using vectors

Imagine this phone agenda will have more than 100 phone numbers. Are you going to declare 100 variables for the numbers? And another 100 for the names? Of course not. Here is where vector fits perfectly. With vector, you will be able to insert as many elements as you like. For using vector inside C++, we must add the library <vector> in our code. We will also need iostream and string.

So, our libraries will be:

#include <iostream>

#include <string>

#include <vector>

using namespace std;

After the namespace std, we are going to declare our vector. They will go outside the main function. By declaring any variable outside main (or any function) it means that this variable will be global. In other terms, anyone has access to them for reading and writing. Look closely at the

syntax:

vector<string> Names;

vector<string> Phones;

The word vector obviously says that these variables will be vectors, but now, look inside the signs.

There is the word string. With this, we tell C++ that our vectors will contain only strings. We can only have vectors of ints, of string, or any. You cannot mix data types in a single vector. Now, we will write our main function. Due to the nature of our program, we need to be able to navigate through its sections. The program will have three sections: add a contact, search for a contact using its ID and search for a contact using their name. For accomplish this, we will use a menu that will give us these three options and also an exit from the program.

The main function would like the following code:

```
int main()
{
int sel = 0;
while(true)
{
```

```cpp
cout << "My Agenda++\n\n";

cout << "Choose a number to execute an option\n\n";

cout << "[1] New Contact\n";

cout << "[2] Search by ID\n";

cout << "[3] Search by Name\n";

cout << "[4] Exit\n";

cout << "Your choice: ";

cin >> sel;

switch(sel)

{

case 1:

case 2:

NewContact();

break;

SearchByID();

break;

SearchByName();

break;

case 3:

}

if(sel==4)
```

```
{

break;

}

}

return 0;
```

We only declared a single variable, named sel. Sel (for selection) will be used for the choice that the user selects at the menu. After the declaration, you can see how we declared an infinite loop using while(true). Why do we need an endless loop? Because the program will continue its execution until.. well, we don't know. Inside our loop, there are the cout lines. In here, we show a little title to the user, "Agenda++" followed by two line jumps. And the four following couts are used for telling the user that there are four different choices in the program. By selecting anyone of these, the program will know where to go. Next to this, we left the program to the user, where he will introduce its selections.

That selection falls into the switch statement. If the user selects 1, the program will go into the NewContact() function.

Functions In C++ are a way of modeling the program. Not all the code is written inside the main function because it would be very difficult to follow and also to imagine how all of the piece of code connect themselves. Instead, we divide the program into small modules, where each one takes care of a single task.

Important note: In the code, the main function must be the last function. Write all of the following functions in lines before main.

In this example, the function NewContact() has the job to request the user to give a new name and a new phone, like this:

```cpp
void NewContact()

{

string name;

string phone;

cout << "\n\nEnter a name for the contact: ";

cin >> name;

cout << "Enter the phone for this contact: ";

cin >> phone;

cout << "The ID for this contact will be " << Names.size() <<

"\n\n";

Names.push_back(name);

Phones.push_back(phone);
```

Look how the function starts, it is very similar to the main function. The word void means that this function does not return anything (right now may sound confusing, but you'll get it soon). After the brace is where the function code actually starts. The first thing we do is to declare a couple of string, one named name and the other one phone. These string will be used for the input from the user.

We request the user to enter the name and the phone for the new contact. Now that we have it, we must assing this contact its ID number. Remember classes? The vector contains a property named size(), which tells us how many elements does the vector holds. In this case, we assign the ID as the current size.

After that, we use another great tool from vector, actually the most basic one: push back. Imagine a vector like a deck of cards. The function push back will add a new element at the back of the actual deck.

For this example, we add at the end of our name vector the value that the user entered. The same thing for the the phones. And now we have both values in our vectors.

Now that we have our function for inserting values, we need to retrieve them from their storage.

That is where the functions for search will be implemented.

For the ID, our function will be like this:

void SearchByID()

{

int value;

cout << "\n\nEnter the ID of the contact to search: ";

cin >> value;

```
if(value >= Names.size())

{

cout << "This ID does not exist\n\n";

return;

}

cout << "Information for contact " << value << "\n";

cout << "Name: " << Names[value] << "\n";

cout << "Phone: " << Phones[value] << "\n";
```

Again, first off everything, we write the function name, in this case will be SearchByID. After this, the variable value will contain the value that the user wants to search. Before making any search, we must assure that this variable is withing range from our vector. What does this means? Well, suppose we have a vector with 5 elements and the user inputs the number 8. What should we do?

We already know that our vector is 5 elements long, so, if the number that the user enters in the search is equal or greater than the size of our vector, then it will be of range.

This is implemented using the if shown on the function. If this certain condition occurs, it will show a message on our program stating that "This ID does not exist" followed by the return keyword.

The function of return is to terminate the function. In order to NOT execute any search, we must exit the function before it reaches the next code. Because of this, the return keyword is added and after the cout inside our condition, the function immediately ends and return to the main function.

If the value entered by the user is a valid one, then, it will locate the information. Notice how in the last two couts we use the "[]" operator. This is called an index and it is used to differentiate values within the vector. It goes from 0 up to size() -1.

Let's suppose that the user enters for name the values: John, Michael, Sean. And for the phones:

111111, 333333, 555555. Then, our vectors would be like this:

Names = John, Michael, Sean

Phones: 111111,333333,555555

If we want to retrieve the information, Names[0] would be John; Names[1] would be Michael and

Names[2] would be Sean. The same occurs with the phones. So here, we use the ID given to retrieve these data and the show it to the screen.

Finally, we'll go to the search function but this time we will search by the name of the contact we want to find. The code for this function looks like this:

```
void SearchByName()
{
bool found = false;
```

```
string name;

cout << "\n\nEnter the name to search: ";

cin >> name;

for(int i = 0; i != Names.size(); i++)

{

if(Names[i] == name)

{

cout << "Name: " << Names[i] << "\n";

cout << "Phone: " << Phones[i] << "\n";

found = true;

}

}

if(!found)

{
```

Here we declared two variables, found and name. Name will be the string that we want to look for and found is a variable of data type BOOL (those that are only true or false) and will tell us if our search was either successful or failed.

First, we request the user to enter the name to search for and after this, we will use a for loop to

cycle through all of the elements. The accumulator is started, like usual, at zero. Now, notice how our condition has changed:

I != Names.size()

Thanks to this little function named size(), our for loop will be able to go through all the elements until it reaches the end of itself. With this size() function, we can be completely sure that we do not go out of bound of our vector. If you do not use size(), then you will have some kind of risk looping through the vector. If this error happens, it will be on runtime and the compiler wont warn you about this, so it's safer to use the size function.

Each lap that our loop has will compare the string at the I position in the vector with the string that the user entered. If both strings are equal, then it will show the user the name and the phone for that contact. Also, it will change the state of found to true.

After exiting the loop, it will check if the variable found is false. The exclamation sign at the start of the variable means a negation (NOT) so, if found IS false, then the flow will fall on to the block of code of the if and show the user the message "No contact was found with this name".

After verifying the state, the function ends and the flow of the program returns to the main function.

cout << "No contact was found with this name!\n\n";

Conclusion

There is a lot that you have learned. C++ is an upgrade of C language. C++ has similar advantages just like the C language but it has more features. C++ boasts of a steep learning curve which might make it less appealing to a novice programmer. C++ programming is a great language for one who wants to write programs that require speed and scalability.

You have seen that the C++ program supports object-oriented programming. Classes are used to define objects. Also, you learned that the general format of a C++ program begins with one or more header files that have a predefined function and class. By using the #Include keyword, you are able to use these files and permit your program to access classes and functions they define. After the header files, next is the class definitions plus their respective member functions. Next, you declare global variables for your program before the main() function is defined.

Up to this point, you have read and understood important concepts in the C++ language. Although the book has tried to cover everything, there are at least some topics that are not covered. However, this should not be your last book to read in the C++ language. To become an expert in any language, you need to read a lot of books. Therefore, you have the challenge to look for advanced C++ books and further your knowledge of programming.

www.ingramcontent.com/pod-product-compliance
Lightning Source LLC
La Vergne TN
LVHW051233050326
832903LV00028B/2380